Ohio—
An Architectural
Portrait

by RICHARD N. CAMPEN

Illustrated with over 500
original photographs taken and
processed by the author

West Summit Press
Chagrin Falls, Ohio

1973

This book was set in 10.5
Melior. It was composed,
printed and bound by
Edwards Brothers, Inc.
of Ann Arbor, Michigan
The Paper is 70lb.
Michigan Matte manufactured by
Plainwell Paper Co.,
Division, Nicolet Paper Co.
The author was his own designer

*cut on the reverse side hereof
illustrates the Old Capitol and
State Office Building
which occupied a site along-
side the present State Capitol at
Columbus between 1817–1852*

Table of Contents

c. 1

Once again, TO HELEN

*whose devotion, understanding
and sense of values has, to
no small degree, provided the
author with the freedom to
find fullfilment in this
volume.*

Warren G. Harding Tomb
(Dedicated 1927)
Marion
Resembling a Greek Tholos, the impressive Harding Tomb is constructed entirely of white Georgia marble. It measures 103 feet in diameter and 52 feet in height. The sarcophagi of the President and his wife rest within its open enclosure. The President died in 1923 at the age of 58.

Preface

The purpose of this volume is to record the best surviving historic architecture in the great State of Ohio and to capture some of the excitement in the work of contemporary practitioners of the building art. It is believed that in so doing a long-standing need is satisfied since no other available work considers the whole gamut of Ohio's architecture—residential, governmental, commercial and institutional—from earliest times to the present day. For over a third of a century I. T. Frary's *Early Homes of Ohio* has remained virtually the only source to which one might turn for an overview of the Buckeye State's domestic building. However, useful as it has been, it does not go beyond the Greek Revival period which had all but expired by the early 1850's. Thus, the last century and a quarter has been almost totally neglected by historians with the result that there is no existing, comprehensive, published source to which either the serious student, the inquisitive buff and/or the interested resident and traveller may turn for up-dated enlightenment.

Furthermore, in the interim, the field of architectural history has greatly developed in our country and elsewhere. A whole new discipline has emerged. The longer perspective which the final quarter of the twentieth century affords, has enabled historians to more clearly perceive the stylistic trends of the 19th century as well as the forces that shaped them. Also, the eclectic buildings of the Victorian age—from the Civil War to the turn of the century—scornfully regarded and unappreciated as late as 1940, have in the post World War II period found their rightful place—even esteem—in the eye of scholar and many laymen alike. The greater professionalism of today's architectural historian enables him to more accurately discern and codify the modes of the more recent past than had heretofore been possible.

No attempt is made in the introductory essay which follows to define the successive architectural styles which have characterized the Nation's and Ohio's building, or to trace the diverse factors which brought them into being. Such investigations have been eminently reported elsewhere* and since, by-in-large, Ohio's experience differs little from that of the Nation at large, there seems little benefit in its reiteration here.

*cf. *'d items in bibliography.

The essay does, however, suggest at the outset how early patterns of settlement diversely influenced the regional architecture within the State during its formative years. It then observes that the architectural history of the Nation, to a surprising degree, is recapitulated in the progression of courthouses in which Ohio, with eighty-eight counties all erected in this interim, is so extraordinarily rich. The same observation is equally valid for collegiate building in the State. Prior to the great population surge and shifts of the recent post-war period, and the proliferation of colleges everywhere in the land, Ohio prided itself in having more colleges than any other state. These were mostly founded in the nineteenth century. Finally, the essay, with an assist from the photo file, touchs upon the plight of our cities and the prodigious efforts expended during the past decade to bring new vitality to their troubled and declining cores.

A great deal of time and thought has been given to the framing of the photo captions to the end that they may be both informative and interesting. Their emphasis is upon building styles and their concomitant forms. It is believed that in their careful review, with reference to the appropriate photos, the reader will unwittingly become a self-tutored, connoisseur of styles as he mentally assembles (from numbers of captions of the same period) the combinations of forms which comprise a style—thereby preparing himself for the ultimate pleasure of recognizing them when they are seen in the field. It is hoped that in this manner the volume will make a contribution to the individual's appreciation of Ohio's architectural heritage. While the author did not set out to write a text, it is not beyond the realm of possibility that this book might prove to be useful as an educational tool in Ohio's schools. Its pictorial content, in addition to recording for posterity the architectural scene at this point in time, will certainly be useful to the serious student and professional.

The organization of the photographs posed a dilemma. This might have been done by any one of the following systems: stylistically, in chronological sequence; by building type (i.e. residential, church, collegiate, etc.); alphabetically by community; or geographically by region. Each has its advantages and disadvantages. Organization by style is at once the most logical choice from the standpoint of the architectural historian. However, there is much pleasure and benefit to be derived from grouping together all building types and periods of major cities such as Cleveland, Columbus and Cincinnati—so that these may be viewed as entities rather than scattered amongst many stylistic categories. Similar considerations suggest that Ohio's ubiquitous, period courthouses, mostly products of the nineteenth century, might better be appreciated as a separate group. So it is also with respect to collegiate architecture where, in the appropriate photo section, an attempt has been made to place reverred campus landmarks in juxtaposition to noteworthy contemporary additions. In the final analysis, compromising with these alternatives, the following major divisions were established:

Residential Architecture—assembled more or less chronologically by building style.
Public and Commercial Architecture—again assembled in stylistic sequence.
Church Architecture—in stylistic sequence.
Collegiate Architecture—by institution
"The Tale of Two Cities"—architectural profiles of Cleveland and Cincinnati generally ordered from the historic to the contemporary.
Community Redevelopment—in which some major urban redevelopments are portrayed.
Bridges—illustrating the more famous Ohio bridges.
Monumentation, Historic Sites, City-scapes

Two indices contained herein are worthy of special mention: The *Photo Index* (by city and town) enables the reader to know at a glance the coverage given to any particular community with appropriate reference numbers. The innovative *Architect's Index*—considered to be particularly valuable—lists the many architects and masterbuilders whose work is represented in this volume. It serves to point out the many nationally famous architects—too little appreciated by Ohioans—who have contributed their talents to the building of this State.

Comment ought be made regarding the selection process employed in assembling the photo representation included herein. The author's original conception was a book limited to the consideration of some fifty-odd structures consisting of a house, a public building and perhaps either a church or collegiate building for each of the seventeen decades since statehood was achieved in 1803. The innumerable choices for each time-span proved extremely vexing. For example, in the residential category in the 1830's and '40's, should "Glendower" (Lebanon) be favored over the Avery-Downer house at Granville or the Mitchell-Turner house in Milan; or should Akron's Perkin's house or Orin Follett's Sandusky residence get the nod? All are landmarks of the first order of importance.

At about the time these troublesome choices were being attempted, a knowledgeable publisher's aid admonished "the more photos the better!" This made sense! If all of the above homes were represented, more people from more communities could relate to the work; further-more, it would then become a visual record of the best surviving historic, as well as much of the most significant contemporary architecture, on the Ohio scene from territorial times to the 1976 bicentennial. Thus, the decision was made to change the initial concept of this volume from in-depth consideration of a comparatively few subjects to one including the broadest possible spectrum of Ohio's buildings.

Furthermore the appearance, at this time, of Marcus Whiffen's *American Architecture Since 1780: A Guide to the Styles,* to which reference is made below, also greatly influenced the content and organization of the book in hand. Whiffen describes and identifies forty distinct architectural styles which "reached their zeniths" at various intervals during the 19th and 20th centuries. These stylistic delineations appeared to provide a structure through which to include many eclectic and heretofore ill-defined links in the stylistic chain extending to the present. Is it not time that the Richardsonian, the Sullivanesque, the Wrightian and the "stick" style—not to mention the Miesian, the modernistic and the new formalist styles—were understood and appreciated by the general public quite as well as the Georgian Colonial and the Greek Revival? It is the author's experience that an appreciation of the best in all phases of our architectural heritage, leads to an understanding and respect for the best building of our own times. The desire to present the architectural excitement of our time—to the present moment—has expanded the photo content of this book substantially with, it is hoped, benefit to the reader.

Obviously in a State as large as Ohio, not every worthy structure could be included, even if every last one were known. This is particularly true of the past quarter century during which the Nation has experienced a population and accompanying building explosion. However, the author believes that the important historic landmarks omitted are comparatively few and that 20th century building is represented by exemplary speci-mens—including, particularly, those designed by architects of note. In ferreting out the historic landmarks a preliminary county-by-county survey entitled *Ohio Historic Landmarks Phase I* compiled by The Ohio Historical Society in 1967 was most helpful. In the identification of noteworthy contemporary designs the advise of the State architect and regionally practicing architects was invaluable. Of course, much of the important architecture of any age is that built for government, for religious observance, and for higher educational purposes. It is not difficult for the discerning eye to isolate these and make a judgement concerning them. (Comprehensive consideration of the Western Reserve may be found in the author's *Architecture of the Western Reserve: 1800–1900,* Press of Case-Western Reserve University.)

Mere age, historic association or identification with a noted individual did not insure inclusion in this work. There are literally dozens of "century houses" which have been passed over because they lacked sufficient architectural interest. Likewise, for example, though Paul Lawrence Dunbar may have been a notable Ohio poet, his Dayton residence is of little architectural distinction—the primary "yardstick" used in making these judgements. Within the bounds of space, and often the avoidance of repetition, we have attempted to be as inclusive as possible.

Reference has been made above to Marcus Whiffen's useful volume. His stylistic delineations at first seemed made-to-order, without abridgement, as a means of structuring this work. However, its numerous categorizations, however accurate, resulted in what was ultimately considered to be too cumbersome a fracturing of the content. None-the-less Prof. Whiffen has left his mark here for each individual building included has a stylistic assignment in the determination of which his system was freely employed. His book is a highly recommended "field guide" for "building watchers."

It is pertinent to note that of the forty individual styles which he establishs and defines (cf. appendix), all but Spannish Colonial Revival and Pueblo have been identified in Ohio. Moreover, of the thirty styles which "reached their zenith" following the Civil War, many had not been isolated or characterized by historians as recently as 1940. No wonder that until a comparatively few years ago, for many, including knowledgeable I. T. Frary and the Federal Writer's Project *Ohio Guide,* the only worthy historic architecture in Ohio was deemed to be that of the Classic Revival period.

Many persons, whether their field of specific interest be glass, silver, furniture, or architecture, tend to become obsessed with the "Century House" and the antique. We contend that there is equal excitement in the contemporary whether it be the stunning, Mexican-inspired library at Bowling Green State University or a multiple, shed-roofed, suburban residence precariously situated on the edge of a ravine. These are expressions of new building techniques, new materials and new thinking about space and how man shall live.

It is probable that never before in the history of this, or any other, nation has man been so inventive in his architecture. A cursory review of this volume (or the forty categories in Prof. Whiffen's work) illustrate that, with few exceptions, the history of architecture in Ohio, as in the Nation, has been one revival after another. The "new formalism," the "Wrightian," "neo-expressionism," "Miesian" and "brutalist" styles are all *new* departures. It is hoped that the present volume will, through its pictorial content, convey to the reader a heightened awareness and appreciation of the new that is good—representing man's unending quest for novel ways of expression—along with a keener sensibility to the old that has stood the test of time.

Richard N. Campen
Chagrin Falls, Ohio
May 31, 1973

Architecture of Ohio

Importance of Ohio's Architecture

The consideration of the architecture of the State of Ohio is important and rewarding because, for 150 years, from the Nation's enthusiastic embrace of the Greek Revival in the 1820's to the present day, building in the State reflects the succession of styles which mark the development of the building art in the Nation at large.

If it was valid to observe in the late 1930's that "the traveller through Ohio will be less conscious of an architectural heritage than he would be in the East, because good examples of early architecture are relatively scarce," as was done by the editor of an abbreviated section on architecture in *The Ohio Guide;** we would question the validity of this statement today when architectural historians are as much concerned with the numerous revival styles which characterized the period immediately preceeding the Civil War (as well as the eclecticism of the Victorian era which followed) *above and beyond* the almost total preoccupation, by many, with Georgian Colonial and Classic Revival styles as recently as the early 1940's.

Nowhere in the Nation is there a more impressive heritage of Greek Revival architecture, in all its mutations, than in Ohio where it flourished concurrently with the great westward migration of 'fortune-seekers' from the Eastern seaboard to the 'Ohio Country' following the Treaty of Ghent (December 12, 1814) which terminated the War of 1812. Moreover, few regions of the Nation possess more varied and numerous examples of the Gothic Revival, the Italianate, the Second Empire, and other styles "which reached their zeniths" at various intervals in the years between 1820 and 1900. In fact, as has been noted in the preface, of the forty architectural styles delineated in Marcus Whiffen's *"American Architecture Since 1780; A Guide to the Styles"* all but a few are to be found abundantly in Ohio.

Furthermore, an impressive number of the Nation's leading architects from 1800 onward are either represented by works in Ohio or have otherwise collaborated on important projects. *Benjamin Latrobe,*[1] for example, is known to have drawn the plan for "Adena"—Thomas Worthington's residence at Chillicothe and either *Latrobe or James Hoban* are credited with the splendid design of Cincinnati's important *Baum-*

*Federal Writer's Project *Ohio Guide* (1940)

Taft house (c. 1820, Fig. 401). The plan finally adopted for the *Statehouse* in Columbus (Fig. 205)—a synthesis of three award-winning designs in which the ideas of the Hudson River School painter Thomas Cole* were most influential,—can be traced to the then prestigious New York firm of *Davis & Town:*[2] (Martin E. Thompson, an associate of this firm, won second place for his design in the National competition; Thomas Cole's plan took third). In the final stages of its construction *Thomas Upstick Walter* and *Richard Upjohn*[3] were retained as consultants. Even *Charles Bulfinch*[4] enters the Ohio scene as the probable designer of the steeple on "Old Kenyon" hall (Fig. #356) while Toledo's *Oliver House* (Fig. #221) is a vestige of *Isaiah Roger's* career.

The not so well known, but highly competent, transplanted Irish architect *William Tinsley,*[5] whose works appear on several mid-western college campuses, is represented in Ohio by the picturesque *Henry Probasco* house (Fig. 417) in Cincinnati's Clifton district and Kenyon College's *Ascension Hall. Richard Morris Hunt,*[6] America's first L'Ecole des Beaux Arts trained architect, is represented by *Clark Hall* (1892, Fig. 337), a lesser work but noteworthy as the initial building of the College for Women, Case-Western Reserve University. The impressive *Asa Bushnell*[7] house (1887 Fig. 91) at Springfield is so strongly *Richardsonian* that the author is more inclined to attribute its conception posthumously to that great American architect than to the successor firm of Shepley, Rutan & Coolidge (Boston). *John A. Roebling's* epochal *Ohio River Suspension Bridge* (1856–66; Fig. 519) served as the prototype for his more famous Brooklyn effort which it preceeded by two decades.

The pace-setting Chicago School[8] took root in Ohio with Burnham & Root's *Society National Bank* and *Cuyahoga Buildings* (Fig. #454) at Cleveland and Daniel Burnham's *Union Station* (1897, Fig. 279) and *Wyandot Building* (c. 1910 Fig. 289) both of Columbus. Louis Sullivan's *People's Federal Savings and Loan* (Fig. 248, 1917) at Sidney, a splendid representation of this architect's work, is one of the jewels on the Buckeye landscape. The list of other nationally noted American architects** of the present century who have enriched the Ohio heritage with one or more works is impressive. Among them will be found: Cram & Ferguson, Cass Gilbert, Bertram Goodhue, William Platt, George F. Post, John Russell Pope, Frank Lloyd Wright, Charles R. Greco and Grahm, Anderson, Probst & White. Of the moderns Harrison & Abramowitz; Skidmore, Owings & Merrill; I. M. Pei; Edward Durrell Stone; Minuru Yamasaki, and Marcel Breuer—all have left their mark upon the face of Ohio.

The above recitation, we suggest, substantiates our contention that the State of Ohio is indeed, a very rewarding place, in which to study the development of American architecture over the past one hundred and fifty years; for from 1820 onwards, as has been noted, the Ohio experience parallels that of the Nation-at-large. Perhaps the only unique contribution by Ohio builders to the vocabulary of American building styles is that evidenced in the first generation of her county court-houses—a design which would seem to have been inspired by the original Statehouse (Fig. 200) at Chillicothe. We shall consider this interesting and comparatively short-lived abberation later in this essay.

*Thomas Cole lived for a time in Steubenville, Ohio
**Cf. architect's Index for associated works

Early History
Patterns of Settlement

In the early years (to 1825) there were pronounced regional differences in architectural styles within Ohio, particularly as between settlements in the southwest, from the Scioto River on the East to the Indiana border, and those in the Northeast. Between these extremities, the architecture across Ohio's midriff also tended to follow a distinctive pattern in these formative years. To understand the geographic and historical basis for these differences, it is necessary to briefly review the origins of Ohio and of the Northwest Territory which spawned her.

* * * * *

Following the Revolutionary War, the jurisdiction of all English-held lands south of the Great Lakes and East of the Mississippi River fell to the victorious Americans. Our particular concern, however, is with that portion of those vast lands north of the Ohio River, then known as the Northwest Territory, from which the present States of Ohio, Indiana, Michigan, Illinois and Wisconsin were carved. Still hopeful of salvaging some remnant of benefit from this forfeited territory even after the conclusion of the War, the British—based at Detroit—encouraged the Indians to assume a hostile attitude towards the pioneer settlers therein. These tribes were quite numerous north of the Ohio River: aroused and fortified by British exortations in their natural resolve to retain inviolate their hunting lands, they successfully retarded the white man's intrusion. On the other hand, south of the great river easier accessibility combined with the less hostile climate fostered the immigration of Virginians and South Carolinians into the present States of Kentucky and Tennessee so that by 1800 the former, which had attained statehood by 1792, had a population approaching one third of a million persons. A comparable figure for the entire Ohio country at that time, could hardly have exceeded 25,000.

Furthermore, and most importantly, massive settlement of the Northwest Territory had to await the cession of claims to the Federal Government which the states of Virginia, Connecticut, Massachussetts and New York held to portions of the Territory by reason of their formative

Charters. This was finally achieved by 1786 when the claims of all parties was limited to the assignment to Virginia of Military Bounty Lands in Ohio between the Scioto and Little Miami Rivers and allowing to Connecticut jurisdiction over a sizeable slice of northeastern Ohio which has ever since been known as the Western Reserve of Connecticut.

Meanwhile, Thomas Jefferson had drafted a document known as the *Ordinance of 1784* which was prospective in providing for the division of the Territory into geographic units, each of which would automatically enjoy the privilege of Statehood upon attaining a population equivalent to the smallest of the original thirteen States. Before this could become operative, however, it was superceded by the enlightened *Ordinance of 1787* which provided for not more than five major subdivisions and established the firm figure of 60,000 inhabitants as the requirement for statehood. Additionally, the Ordinance stipulated that when a population of 5,000 adults was attained in any of these divisions, a territorial House of Representatives should be elected and a Governor appointed by Congress. The 1787 Ordinance also contained a *Bill of Rights* safeguarding individual freedom and property rights. Beyond its original application to the Northwest Territory, this progressive Ordinance served as the basis for the development of the entire Nation thereafter.

General Arthur St. Clair, first Governor of the Northwest Territory, arrived at Marietta, Ohio on the 9th of July in the year 1788—eight months after his appointment and little more than three months after the establishment there, by Gen. Rufus Putnam with his band of Yankee colonists, of the first settlement in the Ohio Country. Marietta then became the Territory's headquarters until Gov. St. Clair removed them to Cincinnati the following year.

Indian hostility continued. In 1791 Gen. St. Clair took personal command of an ill-fated expedition into the heart of the Indian country in Western Ohio where his comparatively small army fell into an ambush and was decimated. It remained for Gen. Anthony Wayne in 1794, after three years of preparation, to accomplish the destruction of the Indian villages in Northwest Ohio and to bring the Indians to terms at the Treaty of Greenville (1795). This successful campaign laid open the greater part of the Buckeye State to settlement with reasonable security.

Within a year thereafter, the State of Connecticut, which had understandably been quite unsuccessful in enticing settlers to the Western Reserve in the preceeding decade, conveyed more than half of her holdings to the Connecticut Land Company, a group of land speculators, for approximately three million dollars. It was not then long before the initial trickle of adventurous pioneers from Connecticut and other New England States became a torrent. They brought with them to Ohio their Puritan ethic, their remembered concepts of New England village planning, and perhaps most importantly, from the standpoint of our interest, the builder's guides of carpenter-architects like Boston's Asher Benjamin[9] which reflected the English designs of James Paine, James Gibbs and Robert Adam. From 1797 onwards these books set the high standards of taste and proportion which characterized much of the early building in the wilderness. Far from being "cop-outs," to use the contemporary vernacular, these pioneers were comparatively well educated persons of strong moral conviction—many of them graduates of Yale College—who recognized the opportunities for the more rapid attainment of success in the western frontier.

Initially, the route westward was an arduous overland journey which, for a man and his family in an ox-drawn wagon, took many weeks. From Connecticut it most frequently traversed the length of up-state New York entering Ohio at Conneaut. Some, however, choose to cross New Jersey and the mountain trails of southern Pennsylvania to the cross-roads at Pittsburgh. With the completion of the Erie Canal across

Monument to the Start Westward
(Marietta)
(Erected on the 150th Anniversary)
The Ohio story commenced where the Muskingum River enters the broad Ohio. Here General Rufus Putnam landed in the spring of 1788 with his band of former soldiers to found the first settlement in the Northwest; and here, a month or so later, General Arthur St. Clair assumed the duties of first Governor of the Northwest Territory.

"Fallen Timbers" Monument
"Fallen Timbers" Monument, located on a bluff overlooking the Maumee River, commemorates the spot where a small army of white men defeated a band of Indians in the crucial battle which opened the Northwest Territory to settlement. They could not then comprehend the importance of what they did here.

New York State in the mid 1820's, this water-level route became a favorite migration artery. The now renowned master-builder, Jonathan Goldsmith,* who arrived in Painesville with his young wife and two baby daughters in 1811 after an overland journey from Hinsdale, Massachussetts, was typical of these earliest settlers in the northern counties. For most, a primitive log cabin was the first shelter in the "promised land." In the south of Ohio settlers arrived at a faster pace because of the region's proximity to 'populous' Kentucky and the shorter overland journeys facilitated by the broad, navigable Ohio.

We have seen that Gen. Rufus Putnam acting for the "Ohio Company of Associates" established the first settlement at the confluence of the Muskingum and Ohio rivers, naming it Marietta after Marie Antoinette. This Association, also composed of New Englanders—mostly with military experience in the late War, made its initial land purchase of 750,000 acres in July of 1787 with Continental certificates of indebtedness then worth approximately 12¢ on the dollar. (Hence the expression-"not worth a Continental"). Yaleman Manasseh Cutler, a prominent member of the Company, whose memory has been perpetuated in naming Manasseh Cutler Hall (Fig. 385) at Ohio University—the first collegiate building west of the Allegheny mountains—served as the agent to Congress in the rather involved purchase negotiations. The Western Reserve and the Ohio Company purchase were, therefore, two major enclaves of Yankee influence and culture in the West.

The following year (i.e. 1788) Judge John Cleves Symmes acting for soldiers and speculators from New Jersey and Pennsylvania, as well as for himself, purchased a tract of several hundred thousand acres bordering on the Ohio River between the Great and Little Miami Rivers, (known thereafter as the "Symmes Purchase")** for a reported 67¢ an acre and shortly Losantville, as the settlement at Cincinnati was originally known, was founded. It developed rapidly, attaining a population of 16,000 by 1826 which in the short span of four years swelled to over 30,000 thus becoming, by 1830, the seventh largest city in the Nation and acquiring the name "Queen City of the West." Some of its earliest settlers were of German extraction and, as we shall see, their numbers increased.

The Virginia Military District, another of the major land areas in the Ohio country, (reserved by Virginia for the benefit of her veterans as a condition of her land cession in 1784) lay East of the Symme's Purchase between the Little Miami and the Scioto Rivers (what convenient boundaries these rivers made!) and extended northwards somewhat nebulously to the watershed between Lake Erie and the Ohio River. It is well to remember that, at that time, Virginia shared a long common border with Ohio since West Virginia did not attain statehood until 1863. Young Virginians Thomas Worthington and Edward Tiffin, early settlers at Chillicothe where Paint Creek joins with the Scioto,—typical of the energetic emigres to this region,—brought a different culture and life-style to the Ohio Valley. Chillicothe shortly became a center of Virginia influence and Worthington, who played an important role in Ohio's quest for Statehood (achieved in March of 1803), became one of the first two senators to represent her in the Congress of the United States. His home, *"Adena,"* (Figs. 10–16) situated on a height overlooking the valley of the Scioto, reflects his Virginian origin and remains today—even as it was in his time—one of the prime architectural landmarks in the State. Edward Tiffin, Worthington's brother-in-law, became Ohio's first governor.

*For historical profile cf. *Architecture of the Western Reserve* by R. N. Campen. Press of Case Western Reserve University
**Symmes daughter married William Henry Harrison, who became the 9th president of the United States.

PRINCIPAL LAND
SUBDIVISIONS

Residential Architecture

Early Regional Differences Examined

The preceeding historical background, noting Ohio's major initial territorial divisions, has been recited to emphasize the diversity in the origins of the State's early settlers for the light thus shed upon the early regional differences in architectural style. We have seen that the pioneers in the North were New Englanders who either came directly to "New Connecticut" or after stopovers in up-state New York communities founded along the migratory routes. This Yankee farmer and artisan was a different breed from the Virginia planter though they shared many exemplary traits of character. The former, when he arrived in Ohio, quite naturally patterned his towns along the lines of the New England communities with which he was familiar to include a public common with a white, frame, steepled church at one end—complemented elsewhere on the perimeter by a town hall, courthouse and school.[10] Adjacent thereto, as his prosperity permitted, he built one-and-a-half and two-story white frame houses modestly reflecting the Federal forms then prevailing in the East. Although occasionally he would employ brick, fired from the native clay and bound by sand-lime mortar derived from locally available limestone, his favorite building material was the abundant wood from the forests which he must fell to create the farm upon which the livelihood of himself and his family depended. It hardly needs emphasizing that he was rugged, independent, self-reliant, inventive and hardworking.

The *Robert Harper house* (1815, Fig. 8) at Harpersfield, Ashtabula County (commonly known as "Shandy Hall") is an unusually well perserved example of the early vernacular frame house in northeast Ohio. It superceded the "bark shack" which his father* had built nearby when the family first came to the Western Reserve in 1798 and there could hardly have been more than 100 families in the entire region. A scant five years later more sophisticated designs appeared on the scene as examplified by the *Dr. Peter Allen House* (1821, Fig. 26) at Kinsman and Ephraim Brown's *"Brownwood"* (c1820)—both of Trum-

*Alexander Harper a Graduate of Dartmouth College and a veteran of the Revolutionary War. Captured at one point, his life was saved by Joseph Brandt, a British Indian ally—also of Dartmouth.

bull County. Either might as well have been built in Connecticut during this transitional period when Federal forms were fading before the Greek Revival onslaught. The stylistic similarity between "Brownwood" and the Ryder House (1823) of Rensselearville, N.Y., a community founded by Connecticut emigres, is striking. The Allen house with its handsome entrance, unusually elaborate window-framing, swag-bearing entablature and interior refinements, while basically unpretentious, stands as the most eloquent statement of the Federal period in northern Ohio—rivalled only perhaps by the *Dr. John Mathews house* (1829, Fig. 28) at Painesville built by the much-acclaimed Jonathan Goldsmith.

For reasons suggested above, the southern part of the State bordering on or adjacent to the Ohio River developed faster than the less accessible North. Quite naturally, building commenced somewhat earlier and took on a somewhat different character. This is well illustrated by considering two of the finest landmarks which remain from this early period, viz. *"Adena"* (1807, Fig. 10) at Chillicothe, and the *Baum-Taft house* (c. 1821, Fig. 401) in downtown Cincinnati. These, too, are products of the Federal period, but how different from the aforementioned in the North!

Thomas Jefferson was President when Worthington, the squire of "Adena," went to Washington to represent Ohio in 1803. Benjamin Latrobe, a protege of the President, was then Surveyor of Public Buildings—a responsibility which, at that very time, included the design and supervision of the construction of the Capitol's west wing. It was thus not at all surprising that the inquiring, young Senator should have consulted with Latrobe, one of the few trained architects in the fledgling Nation, concerning the home he wished to build back in Ohio. Even in his choice of location, atop the plateau immediately West of Chillicothe, he would seem to have been influenced by the visitation of the President's own home at "Monticello" with its spectacular vistas over the Virginia countryside and the town of Charlottesville.

Essentially of Georgian Colonial design, *"Adena"* may well be the sole surviving, authentic example of the mode in Ohio. It is a truly remarkable structure when one considers that in 1806 Ohio was a wilderness; and indeed it was the showplace of the West for travellers from far and wide. The unusually large window panes, the hand-printed, papered walls and the marble fire-places were features at which the local townsfolk gawked. "Adena" has much in common with the 18th Century planter's homes in the Virginia Tidewater which characteristically consisted of a main block with flanking service wings. It differs, however, in not having the usual, spacious center hall extending from front to rear. At "Adena" the principal entrance leads directly into a combination hall-parlor warmed by a fireplace. Behind this is the formal drawing-room providing access to the garden and grounds by means of unusual window-doors (inventiveness reminiscent of "Monticello"). Another variant from earlier Virginia prototypes is that at "Adena" the service wings have been brought in from their usual flanking position to comprise lateral, forward extensions. Missing at "Adena," moreover, are the usual roof-top dormers and well developed frontpiece so characteristic of the Georgian mode.

The salient point is that no counterpart to "Adena" ever existed in the Western Reserve or elsewhere in northern Ohio both because the style was foreign to the Yankee and because none were sufficiently affluent there to build such a grand residence for several decades to come.

Similar observations may be made with respect to Cincinnati's *Baum-Taft house.*[11] The residence of a comparably affluent New Englander of this time would most probably have assumed the two or three story, "four square" form exemplified by Providence's Thomas Boynton Ives or Truman-Beckwith houses of 1806 and 1826 respectively. However, the Baum-Taft design is not stylistically derived from such new England models, but rather again seems to have borrowed from "Monticello." Both give the impression of being single story residences while actually possessing two floors above ground. Both have what might be described as "English basements" performing utility functions with full ground level access at other than the entrace facade. The portico at Cincinnati, with its Roman Doric columns, is also reminiscent of "Monticello" where a broad Classic cornice precludes the delightful Adamesque (ovoid) windows which so enhance the landmark on the Queen City's Lytle Square. It was, incidentally, from the latter's portico (the house has always been a center of Cincinnati's social life) that William Howard Taft in 1907 accepted the nomination for the Presidency. The Baum-Taft house is quite contemporary with the Western Reserve's Dr. Peter Allen house, but they are world's apart stylistically as well as in scale and pretension. The former is a product of an emergent, gracious urban society; the latter essentially a farm house in a region where society meant "getting to the church on time."

Adding further to this early regional, stylistic disparity in Ohio was the early presence of Georgian inspired designs in communities contiguous to the Ohio River—principally, it would seem, at Marietta. Reference is made to these by Dr. Frank Roos whose doctoral dissertation* in 1938 was written at a time when a few could yet be photographed. It is obvious considering this evidence, that the earlier development of the South permitted a brief embrace of Colonial forms which were to completely disappear from the scene by 1820 when settlement in the North finally commenced to "catch fire." Save for "Adena" not one of these Georgian-type designs has survived to this day.

*   *   *   *   *

Thus far, in considering the early, regional diversity in Ohio's architecture, we have focused on the extremes reflected in the building done by the conservative New Englander in the northeast as contrasted with that in the south indicative of the easier and more gracious ways of the southern gentleman. There was, however, between these extremes, another great avenue of immigration into the Ohio country which influenced the architecture of its mid-section, namely, the National (or Cumberland) Pike—the origins of which are to be found in The Enabling Act by which Ohio was admitted to the Union in 1803. It was stipulated therein that 5% of all monies raised through the sale of U.S. Government lands within the State should be set aside for the building of roads to and through it. Initiatives taken by Senator Thomas Worthington in 1807 to implement these terms, lead Congress to the ultimate authorization of funds for this highway to the West.

Starting from the head-waters of the Potomac in 1811, the Pike reached the Ohio River at Wheeling seven years later—work having been delayed by the War of 1812. The lore of the Ohio Canal days (1830–50) has never ceased to appeal to the romantic interest of historians and history buffs. Less well appreciated is the prodigious effort expended in driving the National Pike westward from St. Clairsville—opposite Wheeling—straight as a die to Columbus by 1833, to Springfield by 1836 and to the Indiana line by 1840. The drama of this ambitious project, carried out under the supervision of Army engineers, comes alive in the recounting of it by Harlan Hatcher:#

The Buckeye Country by Harlan Hatcher G. P. Putnam & Sons Co. 1940
The Sources of Early Architectural Design in Ohio. Ms. PhD dissertation Ohio State University 1938

"Bids were let section by section for the road which ran so straight across the State that neither Newark nor Dayton could deflect it—. The activity along the route was tremendous for the time and well organized. The surveyors went ahead setting the stakes. One batallion of axemen felled the magnificent trees in the 80′ belt; another trimmed them and dragged them out, burned them and piled up the stumps; another plowed, scraped and graded, ditched, surfaced and metalled the traffic bearing lane; another built bridges* and culverts and set up the stone mile markers—. From sunup to sundown the noisy bustle went on, and at nights the flare of campfires was lurid across the miles of its cleared spaces. Six days they labored, and on the seventh there was drinking and riotous carousing."

From Wheeling to Zanesville the Pike generally followed the earlier trail known as Zane's Trace authorized by Congress in 1796. There the Trace turned southwestward via Lancaster and Chillicothe to the Ohio River at Aberdeen (opposite Maysville, Kentucky). The Trace, and the National Pike from Wheeling westward, were principal avenues followed by the Pennsylvania "Dutch" (actually Germans) and Scotch-Irish predominant among the early settlers of Ohio's mid-section. As had been their custom in the East—and earlier in the Old Country—their preference for stone as a building material persisted. A few remnants of their contribution to Ohio's architectural heritage, which have more often fallen prey to earth movers than to the erosion of time, still exist. Among these is the *Headley Inn* (1835, Fig. 9) located on old route US40 (the National Pike) in Falls Township East of Zanesville. Its extended, sloping roof, sheltering the front porch as well as the main body of the sandstone structure, immediately suggests its Pennsylvania "Dutch" ancestry. Nearby, in the heart of Zanesville and now threatened by urban decay, is the solid, Greek Revival *Mathews House* (1840, Fig. 55) further attesting to this preference for stone. Lancaster, O. a mecca for the Pennsylvvania "Dutch" as well as for immigrants direct from Germany and Ireland, took its name from the eastern Pennsylvania community. Columbus' *"German Village"* (Fig. 514–15), a restoration project of the 1960's, represents a sizeable architectural vestige of the many German immigrants to that City's south side commencing about 1840. The Gr. Rev. *"Old Brick Tavern"* (1840, Fig. 223) at Lafayette (west of Columbus) once one of many such establishments along the Pike, is virtually the only survivor still serving the public.

Cincinnati, also had magnestism for Germans. Although originally settled by confreres of Symme's from Pennsylvania, New York and New Jersey (many of whom were of German extraction), the direct German immigration which got under way in the early 1830's swelled to such an extent that by 1840 Germans constituted almost a quarter of the "Queen City's" total population. The fieldstone house of *Christian Waldschmidt* (1804), a German papermaker, in suburban Milford (originally known as New Germany) is a present day reminder of the deep German roots in the Cincinnati environs. The large German enclave there was augmented at mid-century by over 16,000 Irishmen fleeing that Country's devastating potato famine of 1848. Obviously then, patterns of settlement facilitated by Zane's Trace and the National Pike, influenced the building styles en route, and if not so dramatically as the differences noted above between Yankee and Virginian it needs emphasizing, the latter were intensified by a differential in time as well.

It is pertinent to this discussion to make special reference to differences in the Greek Revival style as it exists throughout the State. One's initial impression is that this ubiquitous, late phase of the Classic Revival left a greater imprint upon the northern counties than upon those in the south. However, considering the fine Greek heritage at Chillicothe, Lebanon, Lancaster and Dayton (the Courthouse), we are not prepared

*One of the few remaining "S" bridges is illustrated in Fig. #525.

to press this point. Nonetheless, it is probably true that there is a considerably greater incidence of Greek forms in the Western Reserve, where white frame homes and churches in the style are more evident in every township and hamlet, than elsewhere.

Moreover, there can be no question but that the Greek style is found in a greater variety of plans and configurations in the north than below the National Pike. A favorite early northern design—the "temple style"—a-typically exemplified by the *Wooster-Boalt House* (Fig. 62) at Norwalk, appears to have been virtually non-existant in the south. Likewise, variants of this mode, with one or more lateral wings, are rarely seen below Columbus. Another northern variant alligns the principal axis of the house with the highway and places the well-developed Greek entrance on the sidewall—now a facade. In these, frequent use is made of pilasters either at the corners flanking the entrance, or even as divisional embellishments of the facade. (cf. Mathews House-Painesville Fig. 28). In contrast, southern counterparts such as *Glendower* (Fig. 41) at Lebanon and Lancaster's *Reese-Stevens* House (Fig. 34), not only tend to be more pretentious and suggestive of a more gracious way of life, but often assume a square or nearly square plan which is comparatively rare in the north. Moreover brick with stone trim is more apt to be the building material in the South than the white, painted siding which accents the Western Reserve's country-side. Finally, the familiar, white-frame Greek Church with its box tower in several receeding stages—so characteristic a part of every community in "New Connecticut"—is largely missing in the south.

Residential Architecture After 1850

From 1850 onwards, architectural tastes in Ohio closely followed those elsewhere in the Nation—insofar as the economy permitted. The Octagon Fad[12] "hit" Ohio in the 1850's and '60's with greater impact in the North than in the South. The best surviving examples of this comparatively brief experiment are the Hosford-Mesnard house (Fig. 78) built of a roseate brick in Flemmish bond at Monroeville, Huron County, and the frame Higley-Pelen house on route 534 in Ashtabula County,—though the failing Darrow house at Kinsman, in which the hero of the Scopes Trial was reared, is surely of historic interest. A generation ago Painesville possessed a fine example.

The Henry Probasco mansion (Fig. 417, 1859) in Cincinnati's fashionable Clifton district is an early and convincing example of the Romanesque Revival in the domestic category. The City owes its Probasco Fountain, the central delight of Fountain Square (Fig. 434), to Probasco's philanthropy and civic pride. The fine J. W. McClymond's house at Massillon (Fig. 96, 1893), as well as a number of other Euclid Avenue homes (mostly extinct) by Cleveland's Charles F. Schweinfurth, are representative of the later Romanesque Revival sparked by Henry Hobson Richardon[13] whose characteristic forms are so evident in the Asa Bushnell house (Fig. 91,; 1887) at Springfield. It is no coincidence that this famed designer of Boston's Trinity Cathedral (and successors) was called upon to build for Bushnell since Glessner, for whom he had just completed a massive residence on Chicago's Prairie Ave., was a close business associate.

In all Ohio there are no finer specimens of the urban town house than those typified by the John Hauck and Fechheimer-Strauss residences in Cincinnati's central district (Figs. 418 and 415, respectively). The former, built of brewery profits in the High Victorian Italianate mode, is the most impressive facade on once-fashionable Dayton Street. Stately, reserved and formal are appropriate words with which to describe the latter (Fig. 415) in the Roman-Tuscan style, now occupied by the Cuvier Press Club. Carpenter Gothic, Tuscan and Second Empire homes of the post Civil War period abound everywhere in Ohio. Outstanding examples of each of these picturesque styles are respectively: Gambier's Peter Neff house (Fig. 73; c1860); Elyria's Cahoon-Amidon house (Fig. 74; also the Kent Warner house at Wellington—1868) and Akron's amazing Hower-Crawford house (Fig. 89; 1870).

The shingle style, introduced to the East by Henry Hobson Richardson and McKim, Mead & White,[14] was not particularly popular in Ohio; however, Charles Schweinfurth[15] attempted a few for prominent patrons in Cleveland and Bratenahl. Our photo-representative is the Banta-Mc-Donnell house (Fig. 102; 1890) at Lima. Toledo's Edward Follis has obliged us with splendid specimens of the Queen Anne style (Reynolds-Secor Hse. Fig. 107) and the Chateauesque (Rudolf Bartley Hse. Fig. 135) in that City's 'Old West End,'—a present day gold-mine of period homes. Ohio may boast of only one authentic Prairie School house by the hand of its late, great innovator—Frank Lloyd Wright—namely, the Wescott at Springfield (Fig. 159; 1905). However, there are a handfull of other Wrightian structures in the State including a trio of his Usonian homes in North Canton (Figs. 160–162) and another at Oberlin.

Among the wealthy Clevelanders who deserted Euclid Avenue early in the century for a romantic prospect of Lake Erie at Bratenahl was William G. Mather whose "Gwinn"* (Figs. 124–30; 1908)—an Italian villa by the talented Charles A. Platt[16] of New York, is one of the more distinguished residences on the Ohio scene. It is contemporary with the last of the great Euclid Avenue homes, namely that executed by Schweinfurth for his brother, Samuel Mather, within view of Trinity Cathedral (this Tudor mansion long occupied by The Cleveland Auto Club, is now owned by Cleveland State University). While speaking of the great homes of this period, when large fortunes were building, surely Frank Seiberling's Tudor "Stan Hywet" (Fig. 155–57; 1915) in Akron ought not be overlooked. Its versatile designer, Charles Schneider[17] of Cleveland, later showed us that he could handle the Neo-Classic revival with as sure a hand in Shaker Height's E. R. Motch house (Fig. 117; 1924).

The Georgian Revival persistently infiltrated the first suburbs of Ohio's prospering cities commencing with the turn of the century. Orville Wright's hill-top house in Dayton's Oakwood district is a most impressive example (Fig. 112; 1912–14). No one, however, practiced this mode with more assurance and grace than the non-architect, Clarence Mack, in Lakewood and Shaker Heights (Figs. 113–16). This modern-day master-builder's best known work is "Kingwood" (Fig. 121; 1926) at Mansfield for which he was commissioned by brass-magnate Charles King. In the opulent years before the Great Depression, Boston's Charles R. Greco was called upon by tire-man Harvey Firestone and steelman E. J. Kulas to design a pair of splendid residences in the north of Ohio. The first of these (Fig. 134; 1926), closely contained on a beutifully landscaped, triangular plot in suburban Akron, emits strong French signals; while that completed for Kulas (Fig. 150–53) a half dozen years later, with a commanding vista of the Chagrin valley, crosses the channel for its Jacobethan inspiration. Meanwhile, competent Phillip Small[18] of Cleveland, under the aegis of the fabled Van Sweringen brothers, laid out Shaker Square (Fig. 478) and simultaneously housed the tycoons', sister in an expansive English Tudor manor (Fig. 145; 1924) in nearby Shaker Heights.

Little residential building took place in Ohio or elsewhere during the hard-times of the 1930's or the war years of the 1940's when architects were comparatively happy to find employment with the Works Progress Administration compiling the *Ohio Guide* or commanding LST's in

*Cf also "Shoreby" (Fig. 509) built by Schweinfurth for Samuel Mather

the Pacific. The predominant fashion of the post war era has been the "ranch house," undoubtedly inspired by Frank Lloyd Wright and followers, in which all living quarters are confined to a single ground floor frequently built on a concrete slab. More recently, in the 1960's a comparatively few architects, practicing in the affluent suburban regions surrounding the largest cities, have been giving full vent to their imaginations in the design of exciting living spaces on dramatic sites. A number of these are included in the accompanying photo section (Figs. 163–180).

Hudson
North End of Village Green
Hudson has long been considered to be one of the Western Reserve's most charming towns. In this view, behind the Ellsworth Tower—a Village landmark—one glimpses the old Brewster Store, now a bank, and, to its right, "The Elms," Brewster's home, attributed to Simeon Porter, the competent designer of a number of other Hudson buildings including most of the "Brick Row" of the former Western Reserve College.

OHIO'S FIRST CAPITOL, (1803–1809)
CHILLICOTHE

Architectural History Told by Ohio Courthouses

One approach to the study of architectural history in Ohio is to concentrate one's attention upon her courthouses. The pattern for the first generation of these would seem to have been set by the original Statehouse at Chillicothe, Ohio's first stone public building, erected between 1800 and 1803. We are grateful for the sandstone replica (Fig. 200) of it which the Chillicothe Gazette built in 1940 to serve as its office. This was a most unusual building stylistically, and we can only guess at its archetype. In so doing it is natural that we should look to Virginia and particularly to Williamsburg, it's Colonial Capital, since Chillicothe was a gathering place for pioneers from the Commonwealth. There, it would seem that the most likely inspiration was the Governor's Palace with steep, heavily dormered hip roof capped by a ballustraded 'monitor' and cupola. At Chillicothe, the roof took much the same form, but the dormers were peculiarly missing. However, the complete symmetry of Ohio's original, square Capitol building, its corner quoins, its pedimented entrance combined with the roof style, mark it as a Georgian Colonial building. When the first legislature met here in 1803, it was addressed by Governor Edward Tiffin, a transplanted Virginian like his brother-in-law Senator Thomas Worthington whose residence "Adena" we have considered.

A mini-revolt against what was considered the high-handed tactics of the Virginians at Chillicothe lead to the removal of the State Capitol to Zanesville between 1810 and 1812. There again, the government was housed in a brick building closely resembling in form, its predecessor—the original building of 1803. By this time, however, in place of the triangular, Georgian pediment, the entrance was capped by a typically Federal elliptical fanlight. Again, in 1816, when the Capitol was finally removed to the East bank of the Scioto River—opposite Franklintown—the site of present-day Columbus,[19] the statehouse took precisely the same form even more closely imitating Williamsburg's Palace with the inclusion of a rooftop ballustrade at the base of the cupola.

For two decades thereafter, many of Ohio's counties (which numbered 85 by 1849) adopted the style of these early statehouses for their courthouses. One of the earliest of these is the original Meigs County courthouse at Chester (1823, Fig. 201). Considering its square plan (approx. 40' on a side), its window and door arrangement and hip roof, it appears to have been directly derived from the original Statehouse at nearby Chillicothe. But the best surviving specimen of this type is that on the town square at Somerset, Perry County (1829, Fig. 202). Five window bays across the facade (as opposed to three at Chillicothe and Old Chester) suggest that it was modelled after the second Statehouse at nearby Zanesville.

Reference to Henry Howe's *Historical Collections of Ohio* (1889) shows, in a series of sketches executed by the author in 1846, that as many as 32 of Ohio's early courthouses followed this square, hipped roof pattern with cupola atop. Among these were the original structures at Jefferson (Ashtabula County), Georgetown (Brown County), Carrollton (Carroll County), Lisbon (Columbiana County), and Greenville (Darke County).

The Classic Revival is perhaps first seen in the brick (painted white) courthouse at Hillsboro (Fig. 203), Highland County (1834) where the pedimented facade and architrave beneath are supported by four attenuated Ionic columns. The Roman character of these unfluted columns, combined with the arcading of the windows on front and side walls—also the domed cupola—suggest that the Greek Revival had not yet prevailed everywhere in Ohio. The building is, in fact, transitional between the Federal & Greek modes.

The Greek style is, however, superbly illustrated by the nationally acclaimed *Montgomery County Courthouse* at Dayton (1846–50; Figs. 212–15). Built of locally quarrie Dayton limestone, it was designed by Howard Daniels of Cincinnati who adeptly combined the splendidly proportioned portico with a series of Doric pilasters (simulating a peristyle) along the side and rear walls.[20] Within, at the rear, the architect installed an oval shaped courtroom having a comparatively shallow dome with occulus. The ante-room before it contains a pair of fabled, cantilevered staircases which lead to a second floor gallery. This courthouse stands—along with the Statehouse at Columbus—another triumph of the Greek Revival period—as one of the several most important architectural landmarks in Ohio. Other worthy Greek courthouses are to be found at Georgetown, Brown County (1851, Fig. 204) and at Mt. Vernon, Knox County (1855, Figs. 217–18). The eclectic Ross County courthouse (1855, Fig. 216), also that at McConnellsville (Fig. 220), may be regarded as aberrations portending the demise of the Greek Revival style.

There was, quite understandably, a hiatus in the building of courthouses during the Civil War, by the end of which, the Greek Revival had completely lost favor. However, there appeared on the Ohio scene at Delaware in 1868 one of the earliest of the post-war courthouses in the novel Italianate mode (Fig. 227), which may seem "dated" to us with the prospective of 100 years, but which was then as modern as the "new formalism" of our day. Its hallmarks are a 'squarish' plan; bracketed, broadly overhanging eaves, rooftop cupola and paired, round-headed windows. A few years later at Lancaster (1871, Fig. 225) the stone contractors Blaire & Ebner executed a more sophisticated Tuscan design crowned by a massive cornice. Its smooth wall surfaces bear string courses which connect the hooded windows. Far less satisfactory is the contemporary effort at Lisbon, Columbiana County (Fig. 226).

These set the stage for the ubiquitous, Mansard-roofed, Second Empire courthouses which usually come to mind at the mention of Ohio's historic courthouses. Typical of these—and among the earliest of their breed—are a pair by the Cleveland architect, H. E. Meyer, at the sister cities of Zanesville (1874 Fig. 245) and Newark (1876 Fig. 247). Following closely is architect Thomas Boyd's creation at Wooster (1878, Figs. 242–3). The Second Empire style in Ohio, as elsewhere, can be comparatively restrained as is Washington's original Corcoran Gallery of 1859 by James Renwick,[21] or quite flambouyant, as in the style's best, nationally-known example—Philadelphia's City hall (1871–81, John McArthur, Jr., architect). Over the years, Mansard roofs (most characteristic feature of the Second Empire style) have appeared and disappeared under peculiar circumstances on several Ohio courthouses: its occurence in the unusual Medina structure represents an 1873 updating of an existing building; its insensitive replacement at Steubenville and Defiance represents the desecration of these once fine structures. (cf. Fig. 285)

Beginning with the 1880's, the Mansard fad began to fade. Two works by courthouse architect D. W. Yost are illustrative of this; namely, those at Cambridge and Troy in Guernsey and Miami counties respectivly. The former (1881, Fig. 282)—an eclectic building—is a product of the High Victorian period in all respects including its controlled use of smooth and rusticated stone. In the architect's "pride of Miami County" (1885, Fig. 274–5) conceived less than half a dozen years later, the emergent forms of the Beaux Arts style are seen in the grand entrance staircase, the coupled columns and the overriding dome. By 1894 the Lucas County courthouse at Toledo (Fig. 273) had fully embraced the style to which the French academy gave its name. The Second Renaissance Revival which followed found expression in the stately Putnam County courthouse (1909–13; Fig. 263) which dominates all buildings in the agrarian seat at Ottawa. Cleveland's contribution to this mode (1912) by Lehman & Schmidt with its rich interiors attributed, in part, to Charles F. Schweinfurth, is contemporary with the latter. No recitation of Ohio courthouses ought overlook the neo-classic contribution by architects Owsley, Boucherle and Owsley at Youngstown (1908–10; Fig. 257)—the domed interior of which is as impressive and uplifting as the axiom inscribed on its attic: "A Nation Cannot Outlive Justice; Where Law Ends Tyranny Begins."

Ohio was well equipped with county courthouses by the time World War I broke out and architectural commissions in this specialized area have been virtually non-existant ever since—until the recent appearance of the Richland County Courthouse at Mansfield (c. 1968, Fig. 292), the first modern building of its type in a quarter century. Perhaps another generation of similar buildings may be at hand as replacements for the Second Empire models which were so novel and so admired hardly one hundred years ago. However, should a new wave of courthouse building overtake us, it is to be hoped that other Ohians will be more considerate of their architectural heritage than were the commissioners of Richland County who allowed their magnificent Mansardic predecessor to be bull-dozed to the ground.

The author has not attempted to visit every last one of the eighty-eight courthouses in the State. However, it is believed that the photographic coverage herein provides a very good cross-section of those holding the greatest architectural interest. In screening them and their designers, it became evident that the architects of these now historic buildings seldom "rested-their-case" with a single effort. As architects today become specialists in hospital, school and even newspaper publishing plants—each with its specific design requirements—so, in the 19th century, certain architects made a specialty of courthouse designs. As an example, having admired H. E. Meyer's Zanesville courthouse in 1874 (Fig. 245) in the new Second Empire style, it is not surprising that the citizens of Newark in neighboring Licking County should have sought out the same architect to build them a similar one (Fig. 247) a couple of years later. By 1880, however, when Meyer obtained the commission to design a courthouse for Athens County (Fig. 232), the popularity of the Mansard roof was waning. The point being that architect Meyer was called upon to design at least three Ohio courthouses.

D. W. Gibbs is another architect whose name appears on more than a few courthouse cornerstones. His "tour de force" at Washington Courthouse, (1882–84) in what we have classified as being eclectic in design, was virtually duplicated at Marion (Fig. 283). His earlier, impressive, eclectic effort at Napoleon (1880, Fig. 244) while still retaining the curbed Mansard, pointed the way to the aforementioned twins.

G. Maetzel, whose name has also been thrice encountered in the identification of Ohio courthouses, is the author of another pair of "exact (sand and limestone) twins" at Sidney (1881) and Lima (1882, Fig. 240) respectively, as well as the undistinguished edifice at London, Madison County (1890, Fig. 241) which may well have been the final gasp of the Second Empire style in the Buckeye State. Thomas Boyd, whose name is barely legible in the eroded sandstone at New Philadelphia (1882, Fig. 277) is also responsible for the interesting model in nearby Wooster (1878, Fig. 242–43) where herms support a pedimented porch. Frank L. Packard, collaborator with J. W. Yost in the building of Orton Hall (1893, Fig. 373) and the remodelling of University Hall[22] (1896, Fig. 372)—both familiar to generations of Ohio State alumni—was the talent behind the much admired courthouse at Ottawa, Putnam County (1909–13; Fig. 263). Finally, least the reader's tolerance for this line of investigation wane, the firm of Wing & Mahurin of Fort Wayne, Indiana, whose courthouse at Greensburg (Indiana), preceeded by a statue of James Whitcomb Riley, the writer once stopped to photograph, turned up quite unexpectedly in Ohio as author of the "Romanesque Revival" courthouse at Port Clinton, Ottawa County (1899; Fig. 256). A partial listing of Ohio Courthouses together with their dates and designing architects, where known, is included in the Appendix.

THE OLD CAPITOL AND OLD STATE OFFICE BUILDING
AT COLUMBUS (1817–1852)

Deeds Carillon (1941)
Deed Park, Dayton
Reinhard & Hofmeister (New York City),
Architects
Edward A. Deeds, an 1899 Dennison graduate, commenced his business career
with The National Cash Register. Subsequently, with Charles F. Kettering, he
founded the Dayton Engineering Laboratories Company (Delco) where, under his
direction during World War I, the famous
Liberty aircraft engine was developed. The
Carillon was a gift of Mrs. Deeds to honor
her husband, who ranks as one of Ohio's
greatest industrialists.

Ohio Church Architecture

In reviewing the church architecture of Ohio, we again observe that
the progression of styles closely follows that in the Nation-at-large from
the Federal Period to the present day. Lemuel Porter's *First Congregational Church* at Tallmadge (1822–25; Fig. 305), like many homes in
the immediate region, might as well have been built in any Connecticut
town. It is no accident that it so closely resembles the counterparts
in Litchfield and Lyme (Connecticut) with which it is contemporary,
because its joiner had but a few years earlier emigrated to the West
from Waterbury. This church stands alone as Ohio's preeminent existing
example of Federal Church architecture. No less important either historically, or architecturally, is the *Kirtland Temple* in Lake County (1833–36;
Fig. 306) built by the Mormon followers of Joseph Smith Jr. However,
compromising with Federal forms, it is an eclectic building combining
elements of the Gothic, Federal and even a hint of the Georgian
vocabularies. It was a remarkable structure in its time for the quality
of workmanship and material as well as for its comparatively large
size.

Greek Revival specimens are many and varied. *The Chapel* at Hudson
(1836, Fig. 308) by Simeon Porter (Lemuel's Son) is often cited, but
it is not the one most faithful to the Greek mode: the arcading of the
side-walls is a Federal vestige; also, the principal entrance is under-stated.
Cincinnati's *Wesley Chapel* (1831, Fig. 409) was of the period but it lacked
the characteristic "box tower" and the presence of columns or pilasters
in the Classic orders. *St. Peter's-in-Chains* (1841, Fig. 410) also of
Cincinnati, has been cited* as "a most impressive monument of Greek
Revival architecture." Although it is indeed impressive, it most assuredly
is not Greek Revival. The soaring spire is directly inspired by the London
works in Sir James Gibbs (St. Martin's-in-the-Fields) and Sir Christopher
Wren. The interior is that of a Roman basilica. Only the colonnaded
portico is of classic derivation, and its columns bear the stamp of
Roman—not Greek proportions. One is thus forced to conclude that
the truest expressions of the Greek Revival in Ohio's ecclesiastical
architecture are those relatively small and unpretentious, white frame
churches most commonly found in the rural communities of the Western

Ohio Historic Landmarks Phase 1 OHS (1967)

Reserve (Wadsworth, Weymouth, Windsor Mills (Fig. 307A), Florence etc (cf. *Architecture of the Western Reserve,* CWRU Press, by the author).

St. John's Historic Church (1836, Fig. 450), Cleveland's oldest, may well be Ohio's preeminent early example of the Gothic Revival.[23] It is curious that Hezekiah Eldridge, it's builder—also a Connecticut emigré—chose the Gothic mode at this time when, particularly in the West, the Greek Revival was so popular and omni-present. The explanation lies in part at least in the fact that, for Western man, the pointed window has never lost its devine connotation. Thus, in many structures which are otherwise faithfully Greek, we encounter pointed Gothic windows and even rooftop finials (Atwater 1841, Fig. 309; also at Claridon and Windsor Mills, Fig. 307A).

Nowhere in Ohio is the Victorian Gothic better illustrated than in Kenyon's *Church of the Holy Spirit* (1869–71, Fig. 357) at Gambier, though the *Chapel at Baldwin Wallace College* (1872, Fig. 316) built by her German founders, is an impressive statement of the same period. *St. Paul's Episcopal Church* at Mount Vernon (c.1880, Fig. 315) is representative of many similar popular adoptions of Gothic forms in the post Civil War era. Charles Schweinfurth's *Trinity Cathedral*[28] (Fig. 461) together with Cram & Ferguson's *Church of the Covenant* (Fig. 319) and *St. Paul's Episcopal Church* (Fig. 320)—all of Greater Cleveland—typify a re-enchantment with the English perpendicular Gothic at the turn of the century.

The Georgian Revival, too, in the 1920's had such advocates as Cleveland's Charles Schneider,[17] designer of *Plymouth Church* (1924, Fig. 321) in the vicinity of Shaker Square and Arnold Brunner,[24] whose *Swasey Chapel* (Fig. 344) is the most visible landmark of Dennison University. Beyond these, in time, we find ourselves confronting such contemporary efforts as Brooks & Coddington's *St. Stephen's Episcopal Church* at Columbus (c. 1960, Fig. 324), *St. Paul's Community Church* of suburban Madiera (1967, Fig. 326) Cincinnati, and Conrad & Fleischman's present day adaptation of the Greek Cross plan as seen at *St. Jude's Catholic Church* (1965; Fig. 00) in Warrensville Heights.

Synagogue architecture in Ohio ranges from Cincinnati's picturesque and renouned *Isaac M. Wise Synagogue* (1866, Fig. 412) to the ultra-modern "Temple-in-the-Round" (Brith Emeth, 1969; Fig. 322) in suburban Cleveland conceived by Edward Durrell Stone of New York City. Between these extremes is the traditional *Temple Tiffereth Israel* ("The Temple" 1924, Fig. 471) in the traditional Byzantine style where architect Charles R. Greco placed the sanctuary under a segmental dome cleverly adapted to an octagonal drum. Internationally known Eric Mendelsohn designed Cleveleland Height's *Park Synagogue* (Fig. 328) in the International style.

William McKinley Memorial
Canton
Harold Van Buren Magonigle, Architect
William McKinley, one of eight Ohio Presidents, was assassinated in Buffalo before he had served a year of his second term in office. He shared this violent demise with another Ohio President, James A. Garfield, who was shot on July 2, 1881, after having been in office only four months. The Memorial is 97 feet in height, 75 feet in diameter.

Ohio Collegiate Architecture

Collegiate architecture in Ohio, like that of her courthouses, churches and dwellings, also conforms to the prevailing vogue of the periods in which they were built. The buildings bridge every stylistic rivulet from Ohio University's *Manasseh Cutler Hall* (1816, Fig. 385)—a Federal structure which holds the distinction of having been the first facility for the pursuit of higher education in the West—to the contemporary 'Brutalism' of *Cincinnati's Engineering Research Center* (1969, Fig. 343).

Prof. Eric Johannesen[25] has dealt thoroughly with the significant collegiate buildings erected during the first two thirds of the last century (to 1870) (many of which are pictured herein) and it would not therefore be productive to dwell at length upon these beyond making a few general observations. The first of these is that considering its over-riding historical importance and its purity of style, *Manesseh Cutler Hall* must be considered the most venerable landmark of its time. If transferred to New Haven, it would be quite compatible with the older structures on Yale's quadrangle where Cutler obtained the education which enabled him to play such an important role in the fortunes of the Ohio Company. Ohio University is to be congratulated for its splendid adaptation of this building to present day needs without having compromised its inherently good proportions and form.

Most noteworthy among the collegiate landmarks of the succeeding Greek Revival period are elements of the *"Brick Row"* of the original Western Reserve College at Hudson, *Erwin Hall* (Fig. 361) at Marietta College, and *Rosse Hall* (Fig. 354) at Kenyon. Hudson's *"Row,"* consisting of the President's house, at least two brick dormitory units, the Chapel (Fig. 308), an observatory and a classroom building—all in the Classic Revival mode—was as impressive by the early 1840's as the similar row at Amherst College in Massachussetts. Rosse Hall, on the other hand, appears to have been the sole Greek structure on an otherwise Tudor-Gothic campus where Bexley Hall (1839–43, Fig. 355), set the tone for a century to come. *Antioch Hall* (HABS 1852–53, Fig. 329) at Yellow Springs is the most convincing specimen of Romanesque Revival architecture on the State's campuses—and perhaps among all other categories as well.

Why there was no rush to embrace the Second Empire (style) on the campus comparable to that in the county seat, may only be surmised. Certainly, the style's best known survivor (though its fate is in jeopardy as this is written) is Ohio State University's original building, *University Hall* (1873, Fig. 372), which only recently was added to the National Register of Historic Places. Henry Hobson Richardson's influence on campus architecture is seen in Ohio Wesleyan's *University Hall* of 1891 (Fig. 382) and the very powerful statement by Yost & Packard, again at Ohio State University in the form of *Orton Hall* (1893, Fig. 373).

By the turn of the century, the Tudor or Jacobethan Revival came into favor with a host of buildings such as Wooster's *Kauke Hall* (1902, Fig. 391) and Charles Schweinfurth's conceptions at Western Reserve University (*Haydn Hall* 1902) and at Kenyon-*Ransom Hall* (1910, Fig. 358). The Georgian Revival—not to be passed over—seems to have found favor at Dennison (President's House, *Swasey Chapel,* 1924, Fig. 344) and at Miami University (*Administration Building,* Fig. 365). Oberlin's *Allen Memorial Art Museum* (1917, Fig. 368)—a stunning example of the late Renaissance Revival by Ohio's own Cass Gilbert[26] cannot be overlooked in this recapitulation of some of the high spots in our historic collegiate architecture.

Awakening from the lean years brought about by the depession of the 1930's and the Second Great World War of the 1940's, there has been a veritable explosion of building on the State's many campuses since the Korean War—and particularly in the 1960's. The fact is that much of Ohio's most exciting contemporary architecture is to be found on the campus—ranging from Minuro Yamasaki's extraordinary, gleaming white additions to the variegated scene at *Oberlin* (Fig. 370) to the giant, circular *Beasley Convocation Center* at Ohio University (1968, Fig. 389) by Columbus' Brubaker & Brandt. Two modern structures having great impact for the author are the delightful *"Library-in-the-Round"* at Heidelberg (Fig. 347–49) and the formal *Grover Herman Center for the Arts* at Marietta (1965, Fig. 362). The initial encounter with either of these is bound to evoke feelings of excitement and fascination in the beholder. Even as this is written, the "building watcher's" curiosity is whetted by the pending completion of *Cleveland State University's* Library Tower[27] (Fig. 491) (Outcalt, Rode, Kaplan & Curtiss) and the impending dedication of the *George Gund Law School* Building (Fig. 339–40) at Case Western Reserve University—one of Skidmore, Owings and Merrill's few Ohio commissions.

Lisbon's North Market Street
—Boyhood haunt of Senator Marcus A. Hanna.

Ohio's Changing Urban Scene

As one tours the great State of Ohio, her farmlands, and even her smaller towns, removed from great urban centers, appear little changed except perhaps for the ubiquitous shopping plaza at their edge. There, no overwhelming commercial development or population explosion has pushed aside, like falling dominos, the 19th century bracketed, brick and frame business blocks, nor the Grange and IOOF Halls. There, oldsters still pass the time of day on benches in the diminutive park before the unchanged courthouse.

Consider that that once, not too many years ago, there were no dilapidating barns, nor any unpainted and deserted farmhouses which we unquestioningly assume were always a part of the rural scene. Less than a century ago, all was comparatively new: the forces of deterioration had not yet progressed to the point that decay was evident. Ohio was then still a developing frontier—and largely agrarian. It was yet to experience the economic and social forces which induced men, in increasing numbers, to set aside the plow and the hoe for the more remunerative job on the assembly line—in the city.

Her cities developed and prospered following the Civil War when many (even as Cleveland) underwent the transformation from trading centers to hubs of manufacturing and heavy industry. The story of this prosperity spread abroad making them meccas for immigrants from neighboring states and overseas. Workers built their homes in close proximity to the factories in which they found employment in that pedestrian age. Distances were not so large between the abode of the factory worker and his employer—nor were their life-styles so markedly different. As business grew in size and power, labor organized and the separation between capital and labor hardened. Handsome profits, not yet taxed away by the welfare state, enabled managers and owners to build fine mansions at first, as at Cleveland, on Euclid Avenue, then in secluded Bratenahl and finally in a limitless suburbia—mobility made possible with the advent of the automobile.

Thus, geographic lines came to be drawn between the well-to-do, owner-managers and the less affluent workers. The phrenetic activity of World War II intensified the disparity by drawing additional masses of less well educated immigrants, to man the machines, from the hills of Appalachia and the cotton fields of Mississippi. Mergers of giant corporations removed the worker from contact with management. The latter's increasing affluence widened the rift in the life-styles of the so-called "haves" and the "have nots." The working man, thru his Union, increasingly demanded a greater share of the profits and the black man, demanding equality, competed for the available jobs. The city progressively became an undesirable place to live as skilled workers followed managers to suburbia—greatly intensifying the polarization of our society. Finally, even the factories—those not engaged in heavy industry—found the environment of the city unattractive. Thus, the least well educated and the poorest elements of society inherited the central city with its many over-aged, ill-cared-for houses and boarded factories.

Further contributing to the problems of the city, the best retailers found it necessary to follow their 'trade' to the suburbs where great shopping centers were built to accommodate them. This progressive disintegration has forced the cities to look inward, and outward to the Federal Government, for resources with which to renew themselves and make their centers once again attractive places for residence, for shopping and for entertainment. The attempted urban renewals which have resulted are another of the exciting architectural developments in Ohio as we move into the final quarter of the twentieth century.

Cleveland's Enterprising "Group Plan"

There had been one very significant urban renewal project in the City of Cleveland early in the present century under the mayorality of the legendary Tom L. Johnson when the fortunes of the Forest City were at their peak. Some have called it the most ambitious urban plan since Pierre L'Enfant laid out the Capitol City at Washington. The idea of Cleveland's "Group Plan" appears to have originated in 1895 with a young group of visionary architects who, inspired by the neo-Classic Revival at Chicago's World Columbian Exposition (1893), visualized a similar grouping for the public buildings which were being proposed for Cleveland. By 1902, the idea which these young architects germinated, progressed to the point where a Group Plan Commission was organized. Its original members were architect Daniel H. Burnham of Chicago who had been most influential in establishing the stylistic motif of the Chicago Exposition as Chairman of its Architectural Board. Burnham was also known in Clevelanad as the co-architect of the impressive *Society National Bank Building* (1890, Fig. 454) at the northeast corner of Public Square, as well as the nearby *Cuyahoga Building* and the less well known *Western Reserve Building* at W. 9th and Superior Ave.; John M. Carrere, noted New York architect and erstwhile partner of Thomas Hastings in the prestigious firm which bore their names; and finally Arnold W. Brunner, also of New York, who was to be the designer of Cleveland's Post Office and Federal Building on the East side of the Public Square—first fruit of the "Group Plan." In 1911, Frederic Law Olmsted and Clevelander Frank Meade succeeded Burnham and Carerre on the Commission.

Under the aegis of these highly profesional planners, it was proposed in the First Report of 1903 that the blighted area northeast of the Public Square—bounded by Rockwell Avenue on the south and Lake Erie on the north—between East 2nd and East 6th Streets—should be levelled and made the setting for a peripheral grouping of public buildings. This is the area which has ever since been known as "The Mall" (cf. Fig. 485). As we have seen, the first of these was Brunner's Federal Building in the Renaissance Revival style which was dedicated in 1911. Milton Dyer's *City Hall*, employing the same forms astride the northern boundary of the Mall, although commissioned in 1906 was not completed until 1916. Subsequently, the very productive Cleveland firm of Walker & Weeks filled in the open spaces with the *Public Library* (1925) the *Board of Education Building* (1923–24) and the splendid *Federal Reserve Bank Building* (1923). The vast *Public Auditorium*, largest in the Nation when completed at this same time, completes the grouping.

The remarkable thing about the "Group Plan" was that within two decades it was largely realized, The Mall's open space has recently been embellished by Rapuano's *Hanna Plaza* (cf Fig. 487).

Contemporary Urban Redevelopments

Cleveland's Erieview redevelopment of the 1950's and 1960's—extending amoeboidally eastward from the Group Plan—has been slower of realization. In large part this can be explained by the fact that "downtown" was *the* viable and healthy center of the City at the turn of the century; fifty years later when Erieview was conceived, the forces of dispersal and disintegration were well advanced. Useful, existing buildings were condemned and torn down prematurely and with too much zeal—leaving for too long a gaping wasteland at the City's core. Over the intervening years a number of large, modern, undistinguished panel-wall buildings have risen from this wasteland, as though from sparsely sewn seed. Though planned with setbacks and great fountain-bearing plazas, the sense of intimacy and scale which makes such places pleasant oases for rendevous and relaxation, has not as yet been achieved. Perhaps these later-day planners were carried away with Daniel Burnham's earlier exhortation:

> "Make no little plans, they have no magic to stir men's blood and probably themselves will never be realized. Make big plans, aim high in hope and work, remembering that a noble, logical plan once recorded will never die, but long after we are gone will be a living thing asserting itself with growing insistence."

With all its mistakes and errors of judgment—easily identifiable with the benefit of hindsight—Erieview must be viewed as a gallant effort at renewal. As we move into the 1970's, the ambitious plans for newly established Cleveland State University—taking shape in an impressive series of contemporary buildings of steel and concrete—is heavily counted on to serve as a magnet—once again attracting people to the City's center and infusing it with vitality.

Cincinnati's redeveloped *"Fountain Square"* (1970, Fig. 433–35) has admirably succeeded in achieving the intimacy which Erieview lacks. It is an inviting, multi-levelled plaza somehow reduced to a human scale by the gleaming walls of the soaring *DuBois Tower* and other interesting buildings which define it and provide a varied architectural vista. Its central delight is the marvelous *Probasco Fountain* (Fig. 434)—serving as a link with the past and a never-tiring point of visual interest. Nearby, dark marble retaining walls at the plaza's perimeter, serve as convenient seats from which to view the exciting scene—perhaps while lunching on a sandwich from a readily accessible delicatessen. One's pleasure is further enhanced by the designer's attention to street furniture, including an open, wrought iron "pagoda" which seems to await Liza Doolittle with her flowers.

Canton's new *Central Plaza* (Fig. 510) is another laudable attempt to revitalize the inner city and make of it an attractive place to visit. Here, a widening of its principal thoroughfare, for once reclaimed from the omnivirous auto, is converted into a landscaped oasis whose metal tables and sun-shading umbrellas beckon the secretary and sales-girl to an outdoor, noontime siesta. A fountain-fed, rectangular pond thereon doubles in the wintertime as a skating rink at the very heart of the city. This is exciting and this is good!

Akron's *Cascade Plaza* (Fig. 512) and Toledo's *Levis Square* (Fig. 511) are also ambitious efforts, born of land reclamation thru the bulldozing of older buildings of declining usefulness, again with the ultimate purpose to make the central city a place where the "action is." The former approached by a grand staircase from Main Street, has as its focal point of interest, a large, dish-shaped theatre-arena about which are grouped an impressive trio of 'brutalist' buildings. Beneath is a cavernous underground garage for the use of office worker and shopper alike. Toledo's new, landscaped open space (Fig. 511) is accented at its extremities by the mass of *Fiberglas Tower* and a headquarters building of *The Toledo Edison Company*.

Finally, there is Columbus's German Village (Fig. 514–15)—the private reclamation of an old German settlement on the southern fringe of the downtown area. Here, little vernacular, red-brick town-houses with their contrasting limestone lintels have been restored; window boxes neatly installed, brick sidewalks improved and postage stamp gardens neatly manicured to recreate a pleasant residential community, with all the attractive amenities, convenient to downtown offices and shops.

So, as the cities of Ohio visibly explode and commuters flee ever outward in their quest for green, open spaces, a rebirth is taking place at the nucleus where urban chromosomes are busily rearranging themselves. Along with the dynamic developmnt of the many college campuses across the breadth of this great State, this regeneration of the city is the most exciting happening on the contemporary architectural scene.

Fort Defiance
Visit the site of Fort Defiance, at the confluence of the Maumee and Auglaize Rivers, some summer morning before the mist has risen and all is serene. Then reflect upon those days, 175 years ago, when this was the wilderness whence General Anthony Wayne and his retinue left by canoe to humble the Indian at "Fallen Timbers."

Notes

1. Benjamin Latrobe was an English-born architect and disciple of C. R. Cockerell who came to the United States c. 1797. Thomas Jefferson, who became his patron, appointed him to the position of Surveyor of Public Buildings following his inauguration in 1803. In addition to important work on the Nation's Capitol at Washington, he is noted for Baltimore's Cathedral. Decatur House, headquarters of The National Trust for Historic Preservation on Washington's Lafayette Square is another of his well-known works.

2. The partnership of Alexander Jackson Davis and Ithiel Town which ultimately practiced in New York City, was the most important architectural firm of its day (1829–1844). Among their best known works are the Sub-Treasury (Custom's House) at the foot of Wall St. in New York City and the Illinois State Capitol (1837) at Springfield (recently dismembered and reconstructed).

3. Thomas Ustick Walter is perhaps best known for his conception of the Capitol dome at Washington (1850–63); also Philadelphia's Girard College (1833). Upjohn for his St. John's Episcopal Church on Broadway opposite Wall St. New York City.

4. Charles Bulfinch, the author of Boston's golden domed State Capitol, succeeded Benjamin Latrobe as Capitol architect in 1810. Isaiah Roger's fame rests with his hotel designs including New York's Astor House (1832–36) and Boston's Parker House. His Cincinnati hostelry has long since been razed.

5. William Tinsley came to the U.S. from Ireland with an architect's training. Ascension Hall (1860) at Kenyon College, Gambier, O, is considered to be one of his best designs. His work is represented on campus' at Wabash College, Indiana University and the University of Wisconsin. Consult *Victorian Architect,* Life and Work of Wm. Tinsley (1956) J. D. Fobes; University of Indiana Press.

6. Richard Morris Hunt was the first American architect to attend Paris' L'Ecole de Beaux Arts. he designed many fine mansions in New York City, Newport, R.I. and elsewhere. Among his best known works are "The Breakers" (1892–95) built for Cornelius Vanderbilt at Newport and "Biltmore" (1890–95) near Ashville, N.C.—the largest estate in America—for George Washington Vanderbilt.

7. Asa Bushnell (1834–1904) was born at Rome, N.Y. His family came to Ohio in 1845. During the Civil War he became a Captain in the U.S. Army and following a successful business career became governor of Ohio (1896–1900). He was a business associate of Glessner whose Chicago home at 18th St. & Prairie Ave (1886), designed by Henry Hobson Richardsn, is the architect's sole surviving work in the City.

8. Chicago was the pace-setter in modern architecture during the closing years of the 19th century. The Rookery Building (1886) is perhaps the best surviving remant of Burnham & Root's work there while the Auditorium of 1889 is most representative of Sullivan's. (Sullivan & Adler).

9. Although a practicing architect, Asher Benjamin's (1773–1845) larger fame rests in the many carpenter handbooks which he published commencing with the *Country Builder's Guide* (1797). With his *American Builder's Companion* (1826) he commenced to embrace Greek Revival forms.

10. Refer to Photo #508 Twinsburg, Ohio.

11. Martin Baum, the original builder of this fine residence, migrated to Cincinnati c. 1794 and engaged in a number of commercial enterprises of which one was the 1st Bank in the Northwest Territory. He speculated in land as far afield as the "Twelve-Mile-Square" southwest of Toledo created by the Treaty of Greenville.

12. The Octogon Fad was sparked by Henry Fowler whose showplace prototype at Fishkill, N.Y. (1848) was built in this mode. He disseminated the idea in a book entitled *A Home for All* (1849).
13. H. H. Richardson, born in New Orleans, La., attended Harvard College. He passed the Civil War years apprenticed in the atelier of a Paris architect. Returning to this country following the War, his earliest important work was Trinity Church on Boston's Copley Square (1873). His last great work was the Allegheny Courthouse and Gaol at Pittsburgh (1886). He introduced a personalized Romanesque style which has come to be referred to as "Richardsonian."
14. The firm of McKim, Mead & White occupied an enviable position in the architecutral profession from its founding in 1879 to Charles Follen McKim's death in 1908. Among its outstanding works are the Public Library, Copley Square, Boston; and the now demolished Pennsylvania RR. Station in Manhattan (1906–10). Their sole Ohio projects are believed to be the Butler Museum of American Art at Youngstown and the Niles McKinley Memorial.
15. Charles F. Schweinfurth (1858–1919), the most notable architect to practice in Cleveland between 1883 and 1910, was patronized by the Mather family. He is best known for Trinity Cathedral (completed 1906) on Euclid Ave. at E. 22nd St. and for the nearby million dollar residence built for Samuel Mather (1906–10).
16. Charles Adam Platt (1861–1933). Among his many nationally known projects are Washington's Freer Gallery of Art; also the Renaissance villa designed for Harold McCormick at Lake Forest, Ill. (1912). His Leader News Building (1922) in Cleveland would seem to have been inspired by Florence's Strozzi Palace.
17. Charles Schneider (1874–1932) of Cleveland was, until 1913, resident architect for George B. Post & Sons of New York for such buildings as the Cleveland Trust Co. Main Office (c1909); Wade Park Manor and The Statler-Hilton Hotel. The most pretentious home he designed on his own, in addition to "Stan Hywet," is the chateauesque model fronting on the Maumee River at Perrysburg for Frank Stranahan, founder of Champion Spark Plug Co.
18. The firm of Small, Smith Reeb & Draz conducted a large amount of work for the fabulous Van Sweringen's including that at their Daisy Hill Farm in suburban Hunting Valley. They were also the designers of the Cleveland Playhouse on 86th Street.
19. The original plat of Columbus, Ohio was executed by Joel Wright of Warren County commencing in 1812 by appointment of the General Assembly. Provision was then made for "courthouse square" in precisely its present location. Wright, a stolid New Englander who had engaged in Ohio surveys since the Ordinance of 1787, took up Ohio residence in 1806.
20. The exterior walls of the State House at Columbus are similarly accented.
21. James Renwick's Corcoran Gallery (1859) was one of earliest expressions of the Second Empire style in this country. It has recently been taken over and refurbished by the Smithsonian Institute whose original Romanesque pile he also designed. Among his other well known works is St. Patrick's Cathedral on Fifth Avenue, New York.
22. University Hall, the oldest building on the Ohio State campus, was added to the National Register in 1970 and razed in 1971.
23. St. Paul's Episcopal Church (1841) of Maumee ought not, however, to be overlooked. (cf. Fig. 313)
24. Arnold Bruner of New York in association with John M. Carerre (NYC) and Daniel Burnham of Chicago were the authors of Cleveland's "Group Plan" (the Mall) circa 1910—believed to be one of the earliest civic redevelopments in the Nation. The old Post Office and Custom House (1911) on Public Square, made to Arnold Bruner's designs, was the first "fruit" of this Plan.

25. *Ohio College Architecture Before 1870*—a monograph published by The Ohio Historical Society (1969)
26. Cass Gilbert was reared in Zanesville. He is perhaps best known for the Woolworth Building in New York City.
27. The Library Tower and The George Gund Law School were dedicated in the autumn of 1971 and Spring of 1972 respectively.
28. Schweinfurth's original designs for Trinity Cathedral were in the Romanesque idiom.

Index to Photographs

The Photographs

Johathan Hale Homestead (1826)
Bath Township, Summit County
An early brick house in the Federal style built by Jonathan
Hale of Glastonbury, Conn. who first settled in this valley
in 1810. It is now the nucleus of the Hale Farm and Village
operated by The Western Reserve Historical Society.

Homes of Ohio

Primitive and Early Vernacular Structures

1. **Newcom Tavern** (1796)
Deeds Park, Dayton
Log Cabin
This oldest structure in Dayton, and the oldest of only a few remaining two-story, hewn log buildings in Ohio, was originally located on the East bank of the Miami River in what is now the heart of downtown Dayton. It has served, in its earliest years, as temporary courthouse, church and post office. The bronze bust on the plinth in the foreground is that of Colonel Edward A. Deeds, co-founder with Ohioan Charles F. Kettering, of Dayton Engineering Laboratories Company (Delco Division of General Motors). Pioneer limestone home in the background, believed to have been built by William Morris in 1815, was originally located five miles Southwest of Centerville.

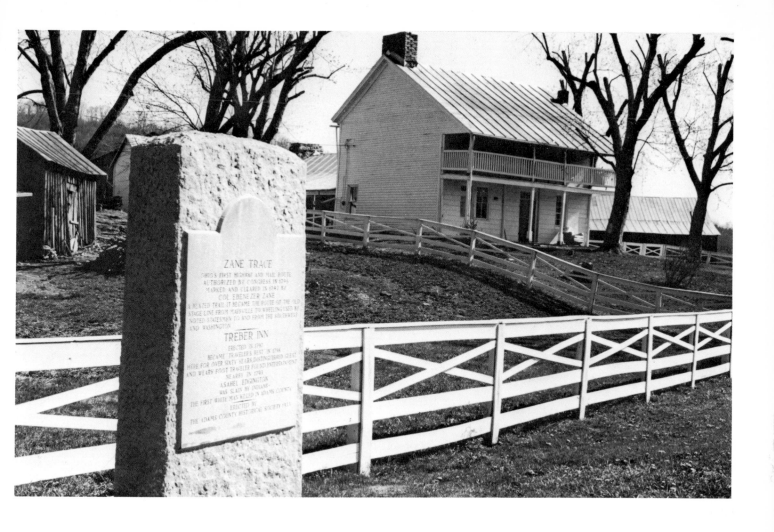

2. Newcom Tavern

Detail—Kitchen Hearth
Segmental fireplace arch is a fairly sophisticated piece of masonry work. The stonework continues to the first floor ceiling. Beyond this the exterior chimney is constructed of a caulked, interlacing of cut and notched wooden branches. Early travellers dined at a table (right foreground) in this "main room" of the cabin.

3. Treber Inn (1798)

Zane's Trace, Tiffin Township, Adams
County
John Treber, Builder
Log Cabin (Under Siding)
Treber Inn, which served the many travelers who took Zane's Trace between Wheeling, West Virginia, and Maysville, Kentucky, on the Ohio River, is, without doubt, the oldest, existing hostelry in the State. The added rear wing is fashioned of large stone ashlars.

5. Tinsmith Shop
Zoar Village, Tuscarawas County
Half-Timbered
The Village of Zoar was founded in 1817 by a group of Separatists from Wurtemberg (Germany) seeking religious freedom. Ultimately, to sustain themselves, they formed a commune under the leadership of Joseph Baumler. The reconstruction pictured is a relatively unique Ohio example of an authentic, half-timbered structure illustrating the type of building frame which prevailed in Europe, as well as in America, from medieval times to the mid-nineteenth century. (Confer also Fig. 29, No. 1 House)

4. James Galloway House (1799)
Xenia
Log Cabin
James Galloway, the builder of this cabin, became an expert scout, hunter and marksman following service in the Revolutionary War. He came to the vicinity of Xenia about 1797 and built this cabin of hewn logs in 1799 at nearby Oldtown. Notable features are the two comparatively massive stone chimneys at either end serving fireplaces on both first and second floors. Access to the latter is gained by means of an exterior stair at the rear of the cabin. In order to better preserve it, the cabin was moved to Xenia in 1965.

6. **Benjamin Rue House** (c. 1805)
Warren County, State Route 350 West of
   Fort Ancient
Stone, Vernacular
Benjamin Rue, believed to have been the
builder of this very early stone house,
served as a Captain in the Revolutionary
War. He applied for a tavern license in
1807, so it is presumed that the house
was built previously. Owned by the Dayton
YMCA, it is considered by the author to
be one of the oldest stone structures in
the State.

7. **Old Stone Tavern** (1803)
Lisbon
Stone, Vernacular
A very substantial stone tavern in the heart
of Lisbon undoubtedly built by a Pennsylvania Dutchman who migrated westward
following the Old Salt Spring Trail from
the Beaver Valley to the Mahoning River.
Principal stylistic notes are the flat
"arches" above the stone window lintels
and door transom. The stone employed
is a local, upper Freeport sandstone.

8. "Shandy Hall"
Col. Robert Harper Home (1815)
State Route 84, East of Unionville
Vernacular

One of the oldest homes in the Western Reserve, "Shandy Hall" is owned and operated by the Western Reserve Historical Society. A remarkable thing about the house is that having been in the Harper family continuously to 1948, many of the furnishings and artifacts from Victorian times, and earlier, are retained in tact. Architectural features are a dining room (banquet hall) addition of 1825, 32 feet × 16 feet, with coved ceiling and wall coverings of hand-painted, imported French paper; also a basement kitchen with a large brick hearth and accessory rooms.

9. Headley Inn (1835)
Old Route No. 40 West of Zanesville
Attributed to James Millis
Vernacular

Virtually the sole survivor of the many Inns which once served the traveller along the "National Pike" in its earliest days. The beautifully dressed, coarsed ashlar masonry is as sound today as when built over 135 years ago.

Federal, Greek Revival and Transitional Styles (1807 to circa 1850)

11. "Adena"
East Wing
The East Wing, housing Worthington's office and waiting room, had a separate entrance. It is known that the masonry walls, sometimes two feet thick, were constructed of stone locally quarried by John and Pusley Morris, also early migrants from Virginia.

10. "Adena" (1807)
Chillicothe
Transitional (Georgian-Federal)
Benjamin Latrobe, Designer
Thomas Worthington, one of the first pair of senators to represent Ohio in the United States Senate, erected this remarkable residence (considering the early date and pioneer environment) from plans developed by Benjamin Latrobe. It seems a virtual certainty that Adena's location on a commanding hilltop west of Chillicothe was influenced by Worthington's familiarity with "Monticello"—President Jefferson's home at Charlottesville, Virginia. The plan and exterior appearance of Adena suggests the Georgian abode of a moderately successful Virginia planter; however, the interior decor is more in keeping with that of the Federal period in which it was built. Adena is owned and operated by the Ohio Historical Society.

12. "Adena"
Entrance Hall

Unlike the typical Georgian plan, where the center hall extends from front to rear, at Adena it becomes a front room. Also, Georgian decor would have called for wall panelling which is virtually non-existent here. Doorway leads to an anti-room providing access to East wing (left) and master bedroom (right).

13. "Adena"
First Floor Sitting Room at Southeast Corner

Beyond the door opening is the master bedroom. Here the woodwork is painted in a vivid rose color; the paper, wall covering features a salmon floral print over a white background. One might imagine Mrs. Worthington planning the menus for her large family of 10 children at a similar desk.

14. "Adena"
East Wall of the Spacious Drawing Room
(20 Ft. × 24 Ft.)
Visual evidence of the refinement within this remarkable, early Ohio home. The simple chimney-piece is Federal in conception. Walnut used in fabricating baseboards, chair-rails, moldings and mantels was procured from local forests—kiln dried on the estate.

15. "Adena"
Original Kitchen
Original kitchen, located in the West wing, was the heart of the house. Here food was prepared; here candles were molded and yarn spun as may be seen at the extreme right. Note bake oven to the left of the fireplace. Stairway leads to a storage loft.

16. "Adena"
Thomas Worthington's Office, East Wing
No doubt many a discussion was held here with Edward Tiffin, (Worthington's brother-in-law) first governor of Ohio, and the many visitors to the pioneer West who routed themselves to this renouned homestead such as Karl Bernard, Duke of Saxe-Weimar Eisenach.

17. "Rubicon" (1816)   (*opposite*)
1815 Brown Street, Dayton
Vernacular Federal
Colonel Robert Patterson, pioneer member of one of Dayton's most important families, built this durable brick residence in 1816 after several decades of Indian fighting and scouting in Kentucky and the Northwest Territory. Two-storied porch reflects southern influence. Now owned by the City of Dayton, the home is used for cultural purposes.

18. Jonathan Meigs House (1806)
326 Front Street, Marietta
Federal
Many of Ohio's great have tread this portal which faces the Muskingum River not far from where General Rufus Putnam and his band of Yankee veterans put ashore in April of 1788 to found the first settlement in the Northwest Territory. Contemporary with "Adena," this brick home, accented by stone window lintels, is a fine specimen, both stylistically and structurally, considering its early date. Meigs served as Ohio's fourth governor, United States Senator and Postmaster General.

19. Orange Johnson House (1816)
Worthington
Federal
Columbus had not yet become the state capitol when Orange Johnson built this brick homestead on the Delaware Road just north of Worthington's business district. Thanks to the efforts of the local historical society, there is no better example of its period and style to be found in Ohio. The brickwork is executed in Flemish bond relieved by the elliptical arch over the entrance and vertical window headers.

20. Orange Johnson House
Entranceway Detail

21. **Mumaugh House** (1805, 1824)
162 E. Main Street, Lancaster
Isaiah Vorys, Sr., Builder
Federal
Stylistically, this, too, must rank as one of the finest Federal houses remaining in Ohio, Characteristic features are the stepped-gable ends, symmetrical fenestration, shallow roof and, of course, the typical Federal entranceway. Brick is laid in the Flemish bond. The front portion of the house (illustrated) was built in 1824; a rear wing dates to 1805.

22. **Mumaugh House**
Entranceway Detail
In addition to the elliptical fan light and side lights, all with leaded glass, the attenuated Ionic columns are typically Federal. The segmental, brick arch is admirably executed.

23. Sherwood-Davidson House (c. 1820)
Sixth and W. Main Street, Newark
Albert Sherwood, Builder
Federal
This handsome "frontpiece" is a feature
of Newark's best known residence of the
Federal Period.

24. Sherwood-Davidson House
Newark—North Side
Essentially a "temple-style" house (gable
end oriented to the street), a surprise in
the form of this two-storied, recessed porch
confronts the visitor whose curiosity takes
him around the North side—a design feature quite unique in Ohio. The house is
now serving as the Museum of the Licking
County Historical Society.

25. "Fighting McCook" House (c. 1837)
Public Square, Carrollton
Federal   →
The lovely portal is a dominant element
of this sturdy homestead of an illustrious
Ohio family. Now owned and administered by the Ohio Historical Society, the
home takes its name for the parts played
by Daniel McCook and his nine sons (together with the five sons of his brother,
John) in the Armed Service of the United
States—particularly during the Civil War
(1860–65). Note the Flemmish bond.

26, 26A, 26B. **Dr. Peter Allen House** (1821)
Kinsman
Willie Smith, Master Builder
Greco-Federal

The Allen house remains to this day, even as it was when built, the most sophisticated farm house in the Western Reserve. The Ionic pilasters, together with the delicate fretwork surrounding the windows, are "set-off" by the flush siding employed. The front entrance entablature is duplicated in the living room mantelpiece. Thanks to Alice Blaemire, who has operated a restaurant in the house for a number of years, the original parlor woodwork, patterned after Plate 26, Design B of Asher Benjamin's *American Builder's Companion,* has been recovered and reinstalled therein (Cf. Figs. 26A, 26B). Peter Allen was the grandfather of Dudley Allen, famous Cleveland surgeon.

27. Wolcott House (1827)
1031 River Road, Maumee
Vernacular Federal

A most unusual home for northern Ohio. One might surmise that Judge James Wolcott migrated to the banks of the Maumee River from the South (though he did not) since the architecture is not in the tradition of the northeast nor of the Western Reserve. In winter and early spring the house enjoys a splendid vista of the Maumee River which was an important travel artery in earlier days. Parlors flanking the centerhall contain sophisticated woodwork; the beauty of the hall stair is enhanced by a graceful curve as it ascends to the second floor bedrooms.

28. Mathews House (1829)
Lake Erie College Campus, Painesville
Jonathan Goldsmith, Master-Builder Federal (Transitional)

This is the best preserved work of Jonathan Goldsmith, the most widely known and appreciated of the early master-builders to practice the builder's art in the Western Reserve. The house exemplifies a favorite plan of the builder; namely, a central temple-style block with recessed lateral wings. The attenuated columns flanking the entrance, the brackets and swags overhead as well as fan light in the pediment are Federal forms; however, the plan is

29. "Number One House" (1835)
Zoar

Vernacular Federal

We have previously noted the Tinsmith Shop (Figure No. 5) which was erected by the religious Separatists who settled at Zoar in Tuscarawas County in 1817. The Number One House was originally intended as a residence for old folks, but, ultimately, became the home of leader Joseph Baumler. It was obviously well constructed of brick and stone by masons from the Old World (Wurttemberg) skilled in the handling of these materials. The two-story portico is relatively rare in Ohio. The House, recently restored by The Ohio Historical Society, is owned by the State.

29A. The Bimeler Cabin (1817)
Zoar

one much used during the emergent Greek Revival Period. Goldsmith's houses were locally very much in demand by the prospering citizens of Painesville which, in that day, was at least as important as Cleveland.

30. **Stanberry-Rising House** (1834)
131 North High Street, Lancaster
Modified Classic Revival

Although highly regarded in Lancaster, particularly for its interior woodwork, it is likely that this house had greater stylistic integrity when built than it does today. When purchased by the Russell Risings in 1937, an acquired Victorian porch was removed in favor of the present Federal-type portico; broad gables were replaced with dormers; a Victorian staircase gave way to a more suitable early American model. In 1957 the house was acquired by The First Methodist Church for educational and social purposes.

31. **Stanberry-Rising House**
Entranceway

Among the notables who have passed through this handsome entranceway were Senator James G. Blaine of Pennsylvania who concluded his campaign for the Presidency at a reception held here in 1880.

32. Stanberry-Rising House
Cornice Detail
A long admired feature of the house by Lancastrians is the decorative cornice with handcarved metopes grouped in an unorthodox manner.

33. Stanberry-Rising House
Center Hall Interior
In keeping with the plan of earlier Georgian and Federal homes in the East, the spacious center hall here extends from front to rear—an unusual feature in this locale.

34. Reese-Peters House (1835)
145 E. Main Street, Lancaster
James Weakley, Builder
Federal-Greek Transitional
William J. Reese, the original owner of
this impressive residence, took as his
bride, Mary Elizabeth Sherman, sister of
the famous Union General, William T.
Sherman, whose birthplace is next door.
Portents of the Greek Revival, at this time
fast becoming the national style, are seen
in the broad cornice-board as well as in
the shape and configuration of the entrance lights. Much of the exquisite woodwork within is said to have been hand-
carved in Philadelphia.

35. Sifford-Taggert House
118 E. Wheeling Street, Lancaster
Federal
The skilled pioneer carpenter who executed this portal employed a great deal of
ingenuity in fashioning the handcarved
arch with decorative keystone which make
it one of Lancaster's most memorable designs.

36. Grant-Haines House (1842)
186 W. Market Street, Alliance
Vernacular Federal
John Grant, not only built this house but kilned the bricks of which it is made. He was a first cousin of Jesse Grant, father of President Ulysses S. Grant. It came into the Haines family through the marriage of his daughter, Sarah, to Jonathan Ridgeway Haines. Here, again, we see one of the few instances of a two-story porch in northern Ohio. It has been surmised that its design may have been brought westward by Pennsylvania Quakers. Also, it is not improbable that Grant was influenced by familiarity with the Number One House at Zoar.

37. Sturgis-Fulstow House (1834)
West Main Street, Norwalk
William Gale Meade (Frary), Architect
Federal
This is one of the lovliest homes on an avenue noted for its splendid residences. It could as well have been built in Litchfield, Connecticut. The modillions under the eaves, the oval sunburst in the pediment, the flush siding of the facade and the slender columns are all from the Federal vocabulary. William G. Meade, to whom the design is attributed, was the father of Cleveland's Frank Meade, architect for many fine residences in Cleveland and Shaker Heights earlier in this century.

39. "House of Four Pillars" (c. 1835)
Maumee
Greek Revival
This marvelous, early Greek house, the finest of its style in northwestern Ohio, was well on its way to oblivion until purchased and restored by William B. Hankins in the early 1940's. The beautiful columns, possessed of a most pleasing entasis, are said to have been fashioned by an itinerant "column maker" who, in passing this way, also fitted a similar set to Lucas County's first courthouse at Maumee. Theodore Dreiser wrote "Sister Carrie" in a basement apartment here at the turn of the century when the house was owned by Maude Henry, wife of *The Toledo Blade's* editor.

38. Cherry-Lockwood-Moore House
   (1836)
Front Street, Milan
Nathan Jenkins, bldr.
Federal
One of the more gracious homes in the formerly prosperous "port city" of Milan is this attributed to Nathan Jenkins. Here, a monumental quality is given to a house of ordinary size by the two story portico with pediment perforated by a semi-circular fan light.

40. Walker-Robbins-Smith House
(c. 1843)
Old Mill Road, Gates Mills
Attributed to Holsey Gates, Village founder
Greek Revival

Typical example of the so-called "Western Reserve" style in the charming Village of Gates Mills, Cuyahoga County. Here exterior simplicity belies the refinement within. Beautifully proportioned entrance, corner pilasters, box cornice and broad eaves boards are characteristic forms of the original house (at right).

41. "Glendower" (1836)
Lebanon
Amos Bennett, Builder
Greek Revival

Originally owned by John M. Williams, attorney and legislator, "Glendower" stands today as one of Ohio's finest historic residences. The original house consisted of the central block with center hall and porticos, front and rear, including five large rooms on the first floor. The flanking wings were added at a later date. A pleasingly subtle, stylistic effect is achieved by the recessing of the facade around the window areas thereby creating the corner pilasters.

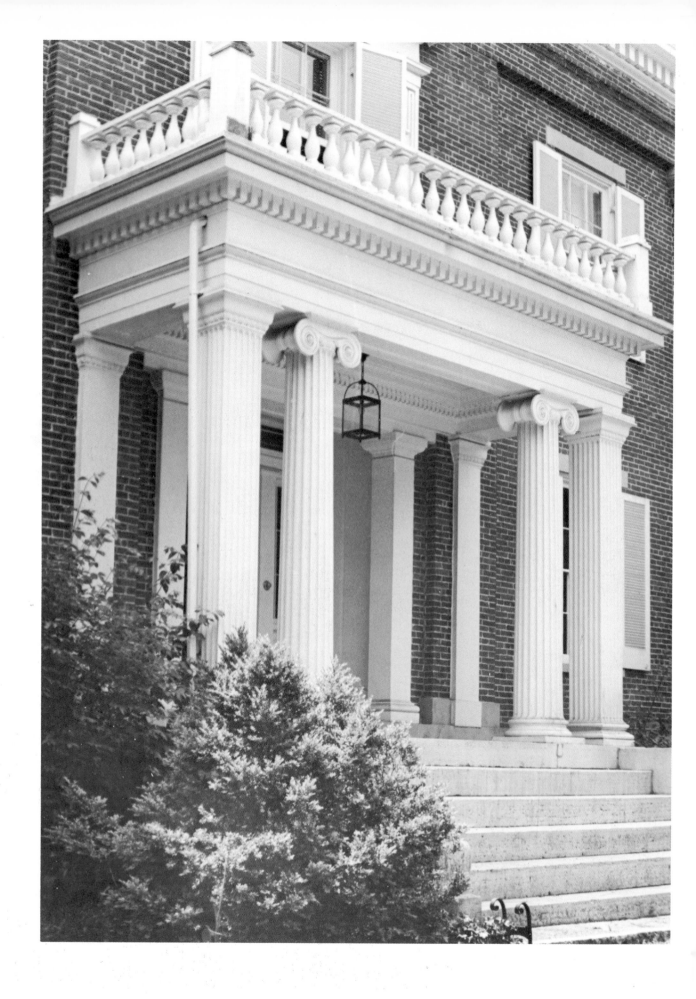

43. "Glendower"
Center Hall—Interior
The masculine quality of the interior woodwork and the spaciousness of the center hall are here portrayed. The stairway with cherry ballustrade extends to the attic.

44. "Glendower"
Dining Room
Admission to the dining room is gained through a front parlor to the right of the center hall. Furnishings at "Glendower" today for the most part represent the work of Lebanon and Warren County craftsmen.

42. "Glendower"
Portico Detail
The massive portico is one of the most 'Grecian' features of the house. Its substantial character is achieved by the broad architrave supported by paired pillars and columns in the Ionic and Doric orders.

45. "Glendower"
Front Parlor
It is here that in earlier times one might have sipped a glass of sherry while awaiting the announcement that "dinner is served." The chimney-piece duplicates that in the dining room.

46. Avery-Downer House (1842)
221 E. Broadway, Granville
Benjamin Morgan, Architect/Builder
Greek Revival
Overall aspect of this Greek Revival heritage of the first rank. Note the three different orders of the columns supporting the portico; flanking the entranceway and at the lateral wing.

47. Avery-Downer House
At Closer Range
The statliness of the Grecian Ionic columns and the intricacies of the highly regarded cast-iron "fence" are immediately apparent.

HOMES/FEDERAL, GREEK REVIVAL, TRANSITIONAL

48. **Avery-Downer House** (*opposite*)
Entranceway

Piece-de-resistance of this important house is the entranceway. No finer composition of the period is to be found in Ohio or elsewhere. Benjamin Morgan, the architect/builder, appears to have invented the column design—Doric at the base and pseudo-Corinthian at the capital. Anthemion motif in the entablature is its crowning grace.

49. **Orin Follett House** (1835)
404 Wayne Street, Sandusky
Greek Revival

Stone homes were relatively rare in the Western Reserve during the Greek Revival period because of the New Englander's tradition for building with wood and the abundant availability of this material. Limestone was, however, locally available and publisher Follett had built for himself therewith a residence which for its stateliness and fine proportions is admired to this day. The interior, consisting of a center hall flanked by inter-connecting parlors and dining room, does not live up to promise.

50. **Col. Simon Perkins House** (1835)
550 Copley Road, Akron
Isaac Ladd of Warren, probable builder
Greek Revival

A residence of considerable pretension in the Western Reserve is this built by General Simon Perkins, founder of Akron and promoter of the Ohio Canal, for his son, Colonel Simon Perkins, shortly after the latter's marriage to the sister of Ohio's Civil War governor, David Tod. It is built of native sandstone on the brow of a hill with historic Portage Path at its rear and a broad vista of the early settlement—now a great city—from its portico. Today it houses the Summit County Historical Society.

51. McLairdburg-Fullerton House
94 South Paint Street,
Chillicothe
Greek Revival
Nowhere in Ohio is the flavor of pre-Civil War Ohio architecture better preserved than on Chillicothe's South Paint Street. One finds there a succession of dignified porches attached mainly to brick townhouses, like that illustrated. The decorative motif on the face of the pilasters directly behind the columns was taken from Asher Benjamin's *American Builder's Companion.*

52. Reeves-Woodrow-Butler House
(c. 1840)
62 South Paint Street,
Chillicothe
Greek Revival
The elevated portico and the characteristic iron grilles at eaves level are the most interesting features of this well-proportioned brick townhouse which is of historic interest for its association with President Woodrow Wilson who here visited his uncle, Thomas Woodrow.

54. Bartlett-Cunningham-Gerber House
(c. 1855)   (*lower right*)
134 South Paint Street,
Chillicothe
Greek Revival
The hand of the same stonemason who executed the porch columns of the nearby Atwood-Wilson house is seen again in this truly unique and distinguished Greek variant. Sinuous scrolls and anthemions decorating the rectangular "pediment" are reflected in the window lintels.

55. Henry Mathews House (1840)
305 Woodlawn Avenue, Zanesville
Greek Revival

The Pennsylvania Dutch who migrated westward via the National Pike through central Ohio favored stone construction. For one reason or another fewer are in evidence today than might be expected. The Mathews house, one of the best extant examples, is in a deteriorating neighborhood and will not long endure unless understanding effort can be exerted in its behalf. The porch is an excellent Doric fabrication. It is a reasonable surmise that the extended, rear "T-wing" followed by a few years, at least, the building of the main block.

53. Atwood-Wilson House (1845)
122 South Paint Street,   *(page 71)*
Chillicothe
Greek Revival

Splendidly executed, tabernacle-enframed, central, recessed porch with fluted stone columns, in antis, dominates the facade of this impressive rectangular brick home. T-wing at rear harbors a two-story open porch suggesting the southern influences at work in this region. Noah Wilson, an early resident, was President of the Marietta & Cincinnati Railroad.

56. **William C. Lewis House** (1846)
Mulberry and Cherry Streets, Lebanon
Ezra Carver, Builder   (*page 72, bottom*)
Greek Revival
The original, classic integrity of this facade
has been seriously obscured by the porch
added c. 1910. It is most unusual to dis-
cover that Hazel Lewis Brooks, the 1972
occupant, is the daughter of the man who
built it 125 years ago. Much of the house's
charm is, therefore, to be found in the many
furnishings and artifacts accumulated by
the family over the intervening century.

57. **William C. Lewis House**
Stair Newell Post
The most unusual feature of the Lewis
house is the unique "Lebanon" newell
post. The stair curves through ninety de-
grees as it ascends to the second floor.

58. **William C. Lewis House**
Parlor Chimney-Piece
Ezra Carver, the builder, took liberties with
the classic orders in fashioning this parlor
mantelpiece. However, the result is impressive. Even the bronze metal framing
of the hearth echoes architectural detail.

59. "The Pillars" (c. 1848)
U.S. Route No. 42, South of Lebanon
Greek Revival (Transitional)
Lucy Boake, whose husband built this gracious home, was a sister to the mistress of "Glendower" immediately next door. The interior plan and proportions are said to have been copied from "Glendower." The appearance of the eaves brackets, over an otherwise properly broad fascia board portends the "decline and fall" of the Greek Revival.

60. Thomas Clegg House (1832)
Jefferson Avenue at E. First Street, Dayton
Classic Revival
The Clegg house is of a most unusual design for Ohio. It is known locally as the first house in Dayton to have had a stone front and the only remaining house in the area with an English basement. If the date of 1832 is to be believed, then certainly the eaves bracketing must have been a Victorian modification.

61. Hurst-Tomes House (1843)
33065 Detroit Avenue, Avon
("Stone-Eagle")
Greek Revival
Long regarded as one of the finest stone houses in northern Ohio, it seems incredible that it could have been built for approximately $650.00. The datestone over the eaves proclaims that the house was erectedby "W. and L. E. Hurst—A.D. 1843." Above is a watchful "stone eagle" by which name the house is sometimes known. The stonework is excellently executed; the interior finish simple.

62. Wooster-Boalt House (1848)
114 W. Main Street, Norwalk
Greek Revival
Originally built as a seminary for girls, this structure was acquired and converted into a home by Henry Wooster in 1855. It is one of a comparatively few Ohio dwellings where giant columns are employed in antis. The effect is imposing.

63. **Nathan Seymour House** (1841)
15 Prospect Street
Hudson
Simeon Porter, Builder/Architect
Greek Revival
A knowledgeable, long-time Hudson resident has called this the finest Greek house
in town. Seymour, whose grandson became President of Yale University, was
a professor on the faculty of Western Reserve College, originally located in Hudson. A spacious center hall, flanked by
the dining room and parlor, runs from front
to rear.

64. **Buckland House** (1853)
Birchard at Park Avenue, Fremont
Greek Revival
Ralph P. Buckland was a Civil War General, a congressman and a law partner of
Rutherford B. Hayes. This fine residence,
built during the final years of the Greek
Revival period, both unique and inventive
in its design, serves to illustrate (with others
in this section) the adaptability of Greek
forms to diverse designs.

65. Mitchell-Turner House (1848)
128 South Center Street, Milan
Zenas King, Builder
Greek Revival

A late Greek Revival home with the full repetoire of Greek forms. The unique decorative motif in the pediment is repeated over the entranceway (Confer Figure No. 66). King's first house in Milan is an undistinguished vernacular brick structure at Wilcoxin and Elm Streets. Following the exceptionally fine Mitchell-Turner project, he appears to have devoted his manifold talents to early experimentation with truss-supported iron bridges—later forming a Cleveland firm for the manufacture of these.

66. Mitchell-Turner House
Entranceway—Detail

However produced, the applied decoration of the Mitchell-Turner portal—consisting of bands of alternating anthemions and Fleur-de-lys—is an eye-arresting, artistic achievement.

Early Gothic Revival Homes

67. Robertson-Powell-Slate House
(c. 1850)
Perrysburg
Gothic

The wrap-around porch is quite likely—and the garage at the rear is certainly—a late addition to this striking Gothic "cottage" which was in all probability inspired by similar designs in Andrew Jackson Downing's *Cottage Residences* (1842). The decorated serpentine barge boards are its most arresting feature.

69. House on Route No. 661 (Est. 1855)
Homer
Early Gothic Revival
A Gothic farm house which also appears to have been inspired by the cottage designs publicized by Andrew Jackson Downing commencing with his *Cottage Residences* in 1842. Board and batten construction was championed by Downing.

70. Howard "Cobblestone" House (1853)
Route No. 82, Aurora
(411 East Garfield Road)
M. Smith, Builder
Early Gothic Revival
The best of a comparatively few cobblestone houses in northern Ohio. The entranceway, with its weighty stone lintel, is pure Greek; otherwise, the forms are those of the Early Gothic Revival. One might presume that M. Smith, the builder, migrated to Portage County via western New York State where, in the vincinity of Albion, there is a cluster of similarly constructed homes.

68. Simonton-Cropper House (c. 1848)
229 South Broadway, Lebanon   (*left*)
Matthias Corwin, Architect
Early Gothic Revival
This, the first house in Lebanon to have been designed by an architect, has been in the same family (without sale or transfer) since it was purchased by Leonidas Simonton in 1906. Every room has a fireplace; the hand-carved pair in the parlor being identical except that one is mahogony and the other walnut. Ground floor ceilings are 13—14 feet in height. Three living room windows, puttied on the inside, have 108 separate panes.

71. Amos House
519 North Ohio Avenue, Sidney
Early Gothic Revival
Enhanced by its elevated situation, this well-maintained Gothic residence is an impressive sight to one approaching downtown Sidney from the North.

72. "Mountain House" (1850)
8 Highland Avenue, Chillicothe
(Dard Hunter, Jr. Residence)
Early Gothic Revival
An exceedingly difficult house to photograph since the land falls off sharply immediately before the facade. Materials for its construction were said to have been hoisted by windlass. Originally built as a beer garden, rows of grapevine were planted in true Rhineland fashion on the steep slopes below. Note the pointed Gothic windows at the second story level; also the Tudor drip mouldings below.

73. **Peter Neff House** (c. 1860)
Wiggin Street, Gambier
Early Gothic Revival
Although appearing comparatively late on
the scene, this house is grouped with the
Early Gothic Revival since the steep, decorated gable echoes the influence of earlier Gothic residences such as Alexander
Jackson Davis' famous Rotch House (1846)
of New Bedford, Massachusetts. Its ornate,
but delightful porch suggests the Gothic
fantasies of Horace Walpole's "Strawberry
Hill" (Twickenham)

Public Square, Troy, Miami County
David's Store was originally built in 1855;
however, the extra floor with Mansard roof
was added in 1872.

The Tuscan and/or Italianate Mode. The Octogon Fad

74. Cahoon-Amidon House (c. 1848)
38369 Cleveland-Elyria Road
North Ridgeville ←
Tuscan
The Tuscan (and Italian Villa) were other picturesque styles popularized by the collaboration of Andrew Jackson Downing (landscape gardner, author) and Alexander Jackson Davis (architect). Rectilinear form, slightly pitched roof, bracketed, projecting eaves and round-headed windows are telltale forms—all present here. More pretentious models usually incorporated an asymmetrically positioned square tower or a rooftop, glazed belvedere.

75. Sherman House State Memorial (1811, 1845)
137 East Main Street,
Lancaster
(National Historic Landmark)
Victorian Italianate
From these relatively simple beginnings a great General, William T. Sherman, and a United States Senator, John Sherman, strode forth upon the national scene. The house has obviously undergone successive remodellings including, it would appear, some "Victorization" following the Sherman family's departure in 1844. (In this connection, consider particularly the window architraves, the door design; also that of the porch.)

76. Drury House (1856)
420 South Market Street, Troy
Modified Tuscan
The porch addition of 1913 is so overwhelming that many might question (with good reason) the Tuscan label. However, looking beyond the porch upon the broad eaves with their paired brackets, and noting the rounded window heads, the stylistic assignment seems more plausible. The original walls were—and are—of brick! The house is one of Troy's more impressive period-pieces.

77. Taylor-Graven House (c. 1870)
Loudonville
Italianate Style
A splendid rendition of the Italian villa style with a fence-enclosed belvedere in place of the tower which is frequently a feature of such buildings. Hoodmolds over the side windows suggest that originally all windows were so adorned. An unfortunate, pillared, two-story portico addition to the facade made its appearance in the summer of '72.

78. Hosford-Mesnard Octogon House (c. 1862)
U.S. Route No. 20,
Monroeville →
Octogon
The handsomest and best preserved of numerous Octogon houses built in Ohio circa 1860. The "fad" was set off by Orson Fowler's book, *A Home For All or The Gravel And Octogon Mode of Building,* which claimed more living space for the same length of wall than could be obtained in the conventional square or rectangular configuration. The rooms are rectangular with the leftover spaces given to closets and storage. A central stair ascends from basement to cupola from which a fine view is obtained. The uniformly 18 foot long sidewalls are 12 inches thick—the bricks being handsomely laid in the Flemmish bond.

79. Octogonal Schoolhouse (c. 1831)
Sinking Spring (Adams County) →
Octogon
Another, similar octogonal schoolhouse exists at Florence (Erie County) in the Western Reserve. Outstanding stylistic note here is the fine corbelling at the eaves.

High Victorian, Second Empire and Eclectic Homes

"Downtown" Granville
A familiar sight to generations of "Dennisonians." With projecting cornices like these, who needs a covered walkway?

80. **Russell-Cooper House** (c. 1850; c. 1875)
115 Gambier Street, Mount Vernon
High Victorian Gothic
Ohio's counterpart to Maine's famous "Wedding Cake" house. A real eye-stopper! Colonel Cooper and his wife (formerly a Russell) acquired this home and greatly modified its exterior appearance following Civil War service and six years in Washington as a Congressman. It is now owned by a granddaughter of Colonel Cooper. In 1970 the body of the house was painted a vivid yellow and the trim white.

81. Morris Sharp House (1875)
East End, Court Street,
Washington Courthouse
(Fayette County Historical Center)
High Victorian Gothic
"Banker Sharp declared he was going to build the 'show place' of Washington Courthouse and now the folks tell us *it still is*"—writes B. E. Kelley, Secretary, Fayette County Historical Society. An unusual feature of the house is an iron, spiral stairway, with golden treads, connecting the second and third floors, which has come to be known as the "golden stairs." First floor ceilings are 12 feet in height. The house combines in actuality, forms of the Italian villa and High Victorian Gothic modes. The tower is capped by a dormered Mansard.

82. Harris House (c. 1870)
241 East Front Street, Perrysburg
High Victorian Italianate
Eye-arresting features of this post-Civil War home, from whose rear windows the Maumee River can be viewed, are the ornate porches, front and side, and the distinctive limestone window lintels which contrast so markedly with its red brick fabric. Fireplaces appear always to have been fired with locally produced gas—the base of many Wood county fortunes—never wood. The roof style is a "compromised" Mansard ubiquitously observed in this region.

83. Anton Brewer House (c. 1830; c. 1875)
249 Lincolnway West, Lisbon
Eclectic
This is a curious house, stylistically. A rear, two-story wing is believed to have been built in the late 1820's; the front portion, including the ornate, Victorian porch and Mansard roof seen in our photo, was undoubtedly added by S. Doughton who occupied it between 1864 and 1895. The only Second Empire feature is the Mansard roof. All-in-all, it is the most impressive home in the central section of Lisbon today.

84. Anton Brewer House
Porch
The porch, a most interesting specimen of its period, derives much of its character from the ornate Corinthian columns and the carved brackets which support it.

85. "Spiegel Grove" (1859, c. 1878)
1337 Hayes Avenue, Fremont
D. L. June, Builder
(Registered National Historical Landmark)
Eclectic
That potion of the house under the nearest gable was built in 1859 as a summer home by Sardis Birchard, an uncle of President Rutherford B. Hayes. Hayes inherited the estate in 1873 when extensive additions were made. The State of Ohio acquired the property in 1909. Since Rutherford B. Hayes was Governor of Ohio between 1876–77 and President of the United States between 1877–1881, much history was made here. Tudor, Tuscan, High Victorian and even Shingle style forms are discernible in the conglomerate. The house is open to visitation.

86. "Spiegel Grove"
White House Gates
To gain admission to "Spiegel Grove" one passes through gates which during Hayes' administration served a similar function at the White House in Washington.

88. Christian Gerber House (1872)
2413 Collingwood Avenue, Toledo
Joseph Morehouse, Architect
(Now Mary Manse College)
High Victorian Italianate
Some (noting the Mansard-capped tower) might, at first, incline towards Second Empire classification of the Gerber House. However, the window treatment and powerfully bracketed cornices are prominent features tilting the scale in favor of the High Victorian Italianate mode. In any event, it is surely one of the most picturesque Victorian houses in Ohio. It is occupied by the Ursaline Convent of the Sacred Heart.

87. Mary Ann Klingling House (c. 1814; 1850)
203 Silver Street,
Lebanon
Eclectic
It is known that Matthas Corwin purchased the original house in 1814 upon his return from the War of 1812. Stylistically, it was thus at first a simple, vernacular house of the Federal period. It must thus be assumed that during the ownership of Mary Ann Klingling the bracketed cornice was extended and the porch added with its decorative cast iron grille-work so characteristic of Lebanon.

90. **House Northwest Corner of Church and North King Streets** (Est. 1875)

Xenia

Eclectic

A massive, Mansard-capped tower predominates over this impressive mansion with other forms suggestive of the Italian Villa and High Victorian Italianate modes. The arcaded stone porch, quite probably a later addition, reflects the Romanesque Revival sparked by Henry Hobson Richardson.

89. **Hower-Crawford House** (1869-71)

Fir Hill, Akron

Second Empire

John H. Hower, an Akron Industrialist acting as his own contractor and designer, built here another of the more impressive Victorian residences in Ohio. From the entrance hall a great, cantilevered walnut staircase ascends through four floors to the tower from which an exciting view of the developing City was had. Beyond this front hall one enters a central, octogonal "distribution" hall from which access is gained, through beautifully executed walnut door casements, to other first floor rooms. Now over a century old, the home has to this date been lived in only by Mr. Hower and his daughter. It was, however, acquired by Akron University in 1971.

Richardsonian and Romanesque Revival Types

91. Asa Bushnell House (1887)
838 East High Street, Springfield
Shepley, Rutan & Coolidge, Architects
Richardsonian

Shepley, Rutan & Coolidge were successors to the prestigious practice of Henry Hobson Richardson who died in 1886. This house is so Richardsonian in character that one wonders whether the just-deceased architect might not have sketched the original plans for Bushnell even as he designed his partner's house in Chicago (Glessner, 1886). The cream-white limestone contrasts most pleasingly with the rose-colored stone used decoratively in the window framing and arcading—both in color and texture. Other architectural features are: built-in copper gutters, catch basins under all plumbing and accessibility thereto by means of removable wooden panels; impressive interior woodwork executed by an imported Scottish shipbuilder. Returning to Springfield with the rank of Captain in the Union Army, Bushnell eventually became a power in Ohio politics and her Governor in the late 1890's. The house is the most authentic example of the Richardsonian Romanesque style in the State.

92. Case Mansion (1898–1902)
1717 Market Street, Canton
Guy Tilden, Architect
Romanesque Revival
At the turn of the century North Market Street was Canton's counterpart to Cleveland's world famous Euclid Avenue. This imposing Market St. manor until recently served as the home of the Canton Art Institute. It originally contained 18 rooms including a ballroom with 16 foot vaulted ceiling, a billiard room, a library and an oriental room. The facing of the ashlars and the woodwork were done, for the most part, on the premises. Mr. Frank Case, for whom it was built, was president of the now defunct Harvard Dental Company which introduced the adjustable dental chair.

93. Case Mansion
Entranceway-Detail

94. Henahan-Breymann House (1894)
2054 Robinwood Avenue, Toledo
Richardsonian
Michael Henehan, a stone contractor, built this picturesque castellated house for his own account. It is unique in Toledo's old "West End."

95. Mary Jane Hayner House (1908)
West Main Street, Troy
Allyn Company, Cincinnati, Builders
(Since 1943—Troy Miami County Library)
Norman Romanesque Revival
Most interesting exterior feature of this half-timbered, eclectic house is the cloister-like porch and front entrance. Its gracious and distinctive interior is planned so that the staircase ascending the rear wall is illuminated by leaded windows whose ascendant pattern is observable from a delightful rear garden court.

96. J. M. McClymonds House (1893)
Massillon

Charles F. Schweinfurth, (Cleveland) Architect

Richardsonian

The McClymonds house, also known as "Five Oaks," is in the front rank of Romanesque Revival mansions in Ohio. It rivals, in the opulence of its interior, the magnificent mansion which the architect built in Cleveland a decade earlier for Edward Everett (northeastern corner of Euclid Avenue at East 40th Street). In 1878, six years after his marriage to Flora Russell, McClymonds became Secretary-Treasurer of Massillon's Russell Company, manufacturers of farm and sawmill equipment. 96A J. M. McClymond House—detail of window at right of arcaded porch. 96B J. M. McClymond House—side entrance detail

97. J. M. McClymonds House

Walls of the great stairhall and landing are painted red and accented by shields in gold leaf with acorns and oak leaves. The stairway is of oak with a solid mahongony bannister. Carved, oak lions sit in varying attitudes atop the newel and corner posts. Visible at the right is a portion of a sizeable Tiffany window.

98. J. M. McClymonds House

Central Hall viewed from the stair landing. Note the paired asymmetrical columns (one octogonal, the other round) decorated, in relief, with hand carved fleur-de-lys. Behind each pair hangs a bronze Pompeian lamp. Total impression is one of opulence.

99. J. M. McClymonds House

The South Lounge

Bay at front of the south lounge extends into the tower. Above the shallow fireplace mirror are corbelled cherub-supported shelves. The fireplace itself is faced with marble tile. The wood, variously curly birch, white walnut and white-rose teak mahogany, is exceptional for its inherent beauty and the quality of the carving.

100. J. M. McClymonds House
Dining Room
Chimney of the 12-foot fireplace is pierced by a window-niche containing a Royal Doulton vase. All woodwork here is San Domingo mahogany.

101. J. M. McClymonds House
Master Bedroom Mantelpiece

Shingle Style: Other American Innovations

102. Banta-McDonell House (1890)
632 West Market, Lima
(Lima Historical Society)
Shingle Style
The Banta-McDonell house represents one of the last vestiges of an opulent period in Lima resulting from the discovery of gas and oil in the vincinity in 1885. At this time what has come to be known as the "shingle style" was being introduced by such prestigious firms as Henry Hobson Richardson and McKim, Mead and White. This Lima specimen is unusual in that it is slate shingle, rather than wood, which covers the walls down to a smooth textured, yellow brick foundation.

103. Banta-McDonell House
Dining Room—Detail
Built-in buffet and cupboard of hand carved oak illustrate the character and quality of the woodwork. Furnishings throughout have been locally assembled to convey the visual image of a midwest house of the period.

104. Banta-McDonell House
Breakfast Room
The mahogony sideboard in the breakfast room is considered to have the best carving in the house. The Victorian chandelier was originally illuminated with gas from the nearby fields.

105. Edward D. Libbey House (1895)
2008 Scottwood Avenue, Toledo
David L. Stine, Architect
Shingle Style
In addition to shingle covered walls, other characteristics of the style seen here are: the rusticated fieldstone foundation; the "wrap-around" porch; the segmental bay and the relatively broad gable. Mr. Libbey was a founder of Libbey, Owens, Ford Glass Company.

106. Warren G. Harding Home (1891)
380 Mt. Vernon Street, Marion
(Registered National Historic Landmark
Stick-Shingle Style
There would be some justification for calling the Harding home "stick style." However, the extensive veranda (without diagonal post braces), the bowed window-bay beneath the front gable together with the rusticated stone foundation, induce the author to place this vernacular residence with those of the "shingle style"—despite the fact that the only apparent use of shingles is in facing the aforementioned gable. Here, in 1920, President Harding conducted his "front porch" campaign.

107. Reynolds-Secor House (c. 1887)
2035 Collingwood Avenue, Toledo
Edward O. Follis, Architect
Queen Anne
This is believed to be one of the finest expressions of the "Queen Anne" style in the State. Present here are the tell-tale, steep, multiple roofs; the attention to chimney detail; the octogonal bay, and the overhanging upper story—all characteristics of the fully developed style inspired by the work of Norman Shaw and other British architects of the 19th Century.

108. Reynolds-Secor House
Porch and Porte Cochere—Detail

109. **Numbers 801 and 849 (Right)** South Lincoln Avenue, Salem
Stick Style
"Stick style buildings have tall proportions with high, steep roofs; frequently of complex plan and irregular silhouette; the eaves are of considerable projection etc.-" "Verandas are extensive, their roofs being carried on posts with diagonal braces."— Marcus Wiffen, *American Architecture Since 1780*

110. **Tillinghast, Willys, Bell House** (1900)
2210 Robinwood, Toledo
George W. Netcher/Brown, Burton & Davis, Architects
Queen Anne
The wall dormer is Chateauesque and its ogee Gothic window violates the rule that Queen Anne houses "never have pointed, arched windows." However, in other respects this "West End" home conforms to Queen Anne dictates.

111. **Edith Barbee House** (c. 1900)
500 E. High Street
Ashley   →
Eastlake Style
A modest, but unique house in the village of Ashley (Pop. 907). Eastlake designs are characterized by ornament executed by the chisel, the gouge and the lathe rather than the two-dimensional result achieved with the jig-saw (Carpenter Gothic). The house is said to have been built by Toddy Porterfield, longtime resident.

Georgian Revival Homes

112. Orville Wright Home (1912–14)
Park and Harmon, Dayton
Schenck & Williams, Architects
Georgian Revival
Success came quickly to the Wright
Brothers following their epoch-making
1903 flight at Kitty Hawk, North Carolina,
as the result of royalties from numerous
aircraft inventions. Orville lived here for
12 years with his sister, Katherine, and,
thereafter, alone until his death in 1948.
The great pedimented portico, the Palladian window which it shelters, the hip
roof with ballustraded deck, the symmetry
throughout—are Georgian forms; likewise
the exceptionally large center hall extending from front to rear. The Wright estate
originally embraced 17 acres on this hill-
top, studded with Hawthorne trees from
which its name "Hawthorne Hill" is taken.
It is now owned by the National Cash
Register Company.

114. **James McGeehan House** (1925)
13840 Lake Avenue, Lakewood
Clarence Mack, Builder/Architect
Georgian Revival
This Mack conception is reminiscent of
Bulfinch's Harrison Gray Otis house (1800)
on Boston's Beacon Hill. Forty-five years
of ivy obscure whatever arcading or other
detail may be framing the ground-level,
round-headed windows; also the full effect
of the decorative pilasters.

113. **13842 Lake Avenue** (1925)
Lakewood
Clarence Mack, Architect/Builder
Georgian Revival
Clarence Mack was a builder—not a
trained architect. However, few architects
would criticize—most would praise—the
legacy of fine, suburban, Georgian homes
which he has left to Cleveland's environs.
Several of his better projects occur on the
North side of Lake Avenue in the 13000
block. In these, one enters a patrician,
ground-level center hall, then ascends a
gracious, curving stair to the second floor
living rooms. The interior finish (mouldings, etc.) evidences fidelity to Georgian
detail.

115. **John McWilliams House** (1928)
19100 South Park Boulevard, Shaker
    Heights
Clarence Mack, Builder/Architect
Georgian Revival
Another concentration of Mack houses
occurs in the vicinity of Courtland and
Shaker boulevards in Shaker Heights. The
most impressive of these, owned for many
years by Mr. and Mrs. McWilliams, is a
reinterpretation of Georgian forms.

116. **John McWilliams House**
Front Hall
The front hall extends the entire width
of the main block, linking the living room
at one extremity to a beautiful stairhall
on the other as is seen here. The spirit
of this stairwell "in the round," with its
trabeated entrance framed by Ionic columns, is Adamesque.

117. **E. R. Motch Residence** (1924)
19000 South Park Boulevard, Shaker
    Heights
Charles Schneider, Architect   →
Classic Revival
Immediately west of the McWilliams
house is this extraordinary and much-ad-
mired Classic Revival residence by the
architect of Akron's renouned "Stan
Hywet" (Figure No. 155, Jacobethan) and
Toledo's Stranahan House (Figure No. 136,
Chateauesque). Its grand setting befits the
noble architecture.

118. **Julian H. Tyler House** (1897)
2251 Robinwood Avenue, Toledo
Rogers and McFarland, Architects
Georgian Revival
One of a number of fine homes, built in a variety of styles over the comparatively short period of 25 years, in Toledo's "West End." The Georgian Revival was, of course, a re-enchantment with the forms of our Colonial Period. Interesting feature is the use of the Palladian motif, with Gothic tracery, in the living and dining room windows which flank the portico.

119. **Julian H. Tyler House**
Entranceway
A handsome and, at the same time, unique design combining both elliptical and semi-circular fan lights overhead. The geometric, leaded window tracery is quite delightful.

120. **Dunn-Blair House** (1915)
2049 Scottsdale Avenue, Toledo
Mills, Rhines, Bellman and Nordhoff, Architects
Georgian Revival
The parallel has been drawn between this handsome residence and Sir Edward Lutyens 1909 addition to "Temple Dinsley" in Herefordshire. James Gibbs' Sudbrooke House (1726–28) in Sussex near London also displays the same repetroire of forms.

121. "Kingwood" (1926)
900 Park Avenue, West, Mansfield
Clarence Mack, Builder/Architect
Georgian Revival

Charles K. King, born at Calais, Maine, found his way to Mansfield's Ohio Brass Company by 1893 and climbing "the ladder" became President of the Company in 1928. Without doubt he admired the contemporary Cleveland work of builder Mack whom he retained to design this gracious home. It is, however, the gardens, perpetuated by the endowment of Mr. King who passed away in 1952, for which Kingwood is nationally famous.

122. F. C. Mills Jr. Residence (c. 1923)
2603 Fairmount Blvd. Cleveland
Charles Schneider, Architect
Georgian Colonial

Symmetry and extreme width are notable features of this impressive Cleveland Heights home. Fairmount Blvd. developed as one of Cleveland's finest suburban thoroughfares following World War I. A variety of styles enhance its architectural interest.

Renaissance Revival Residences

123. **Leeper-Geddes House** (1903)
2116 Parkwood Avenue, Toledo
Thomas F. Huber, Architect
Second Renaissance Revival
With its giant Corinthian pilasters, modillioned cornice and roof-top ballustrade (removed after 1967), the facade here is not unlike James Gibbs' Senate House (1730) at Cambridge, England. Stylistically, it represents a reaction to the varied ornate forms of the Victorian era just concluded. An authentic Renaissance building would not, of course, have had a veranda.

124. **"Gwinn" William G. Mather Home** (1908)
Bratenahl
Charles Platt, Architect; Warren Manning, Landscape
Second Renaissance Revival
"Gwinn" is an Italian Renaissance villa on the shores of Lake Erie. The house is a jewell and the gardens, created by Warren Manning, are among the finest in Ohio. Although the house, with its majestic semi-circular portico, paired curving stairs and fountain court fronts on the Lake, it is the west entrance which is known to most visitors. One may here observe how effectively the roof-top ballustrade hides the shallow roof. →

125. "Gwinn"
North Facade
One of the pair of symmetrical stairs which lead from the spacious portico to the fountain terrace below.

126. "Gwinn"
North Fountain Terrace
In the summertime one may imagine that it is the Tyhrrean Sea and not Lake Erie which he surveys from "Gwinn's" patio-terrace.

127. "Gwinn"
Lakefront Promenade
One of a pair of watchful lions which guard the lakefront promenade at "Gwinn." A belvedere is dimly visible at the right rear.

128. "Gwinn"
Sculptural Detail
Sculptural detail of a wall fountain on the lakefront terrace landing.

129. "Gwinn"
Library—Parlor (Interior)
Overall panelling is executed in walnut.

130. "Gwinn"
Aspect From Dining Room Towards West
  Entrance
Beyond doorway is a distribution hall
providing access to most downstairs rooms
as well as the lakefront portico.

132. Edward Ford House (1901)
2205 Collingwood Avenue, Toledo
George S. Mills, Architect
Second Renaissance Revival
Remodelling is not always for the worse! It would be difficult to conceive this handsome Tabernacle enframed entrance obscured by the original veranda. Here brown terra cotta trim stands in relief against yellow brick; bowed window bays hark back to Adamesque influence upon our native Federal architecture a century earlier.

131. Tremaine-Gallagher House (1911)
Fairmount Boulevard, Cleveland Heights
Frederick Stribinger, Architect
Second Renaisance Revival
Gwinn's counterpart on fashionable Fairmount Boulevard. Besides a marvelous symmetry, the most notable forms are the loggia-entranceway, the flanking tabernacle window frames and the orangerie-like sunroom (right) which Christopher Wren might himself have designed. The white marble trim, contrasted with the pale yellow stucco facing, cause this house to glisten in the afternoon sunlight.

133. Edward Ford House
Stair Hall
Carved mahogony staircase, ascending in well at center hall's right, would not be incongruous in an 18th century English manorhouse.

135. Rudolph A. Bartley House (1905)
1855 Collingwood Avenue, Toledo
Edward O. Follis, Architect
Chateauesque
An outstanding Chateauesque landmark in Toledo's "West End" now engulfed by commercialism and the heavy traffic of two main throughfares. One might have wished for an entrance in keeping with the architecture rather than the enclosed porch. Otherwise Chateauesque forms are rampant.

Chateauesque, French Provincial Types

134. Harvey S. Firestone, Jr. Residence
(1926)
50 Twin Oaks Drive, Akron
*Chas. R. Greco in Assoc. w. Edw. G. Reed
(Boston), Architect*
Chateauesque
Perhaps "French Provincial" would be a more accurate designation for this splendid residence by the architect who designed a Jacobethan manor for Cleveland's E. J. Kulas at Gates Mills and the Byzantine Temple on Cleveland's East 105th Street. Wall dormers, universal in the chateauesque, are only suggested here by the projecting balcony doors.

136. Stranahan Residence (1925)
29917 East River Drive, Perrysburg
Charles Schneider, Architect
French Provincial
Frank Stranahan, Toledo industrialist,
after making a fortune in spark plugs,
retained Cleveland's Charles Schneider to
design his "maison" on the banks of the
Maumee River southeast of Toledo. The
architect's experimentation with style is
evident when one considers that within
the same decade he designed a Jacobethan
manor for Frank Seiberling (Akron's "Stan
Hywet"), a Classic—almost Greek—residence for E. R. Motch (Confer Figure No.
117) together with the Georgian-inspired
Plymouth Church (Fig. 321) in Shaker
Heights.

137. Stranahan Residence
Garden
Frank Stranahan retained Frederick Law
Olmstead to design his garden.

138. 2787 Fairmount Blvd. (1919)
Cleveland Heights
Meade & Hamilton, Architects
French Provincial
In this splendid residence the architects made a comparatively rare deviation from their preference for English forms. The highly visible, steep roof is here perhaps the most obvious feature of the style. The accent given to the stucco surface by stone quoins adds to its charm.

139. Lewis-MeKelvy House (1928)
28503 E. River Road, Perrysburg
George Lewis Walling, Architect.
French Chateauesque
Situated on the south bank of the broad and gently flowing Maumee River at Perrysburg, the Lewis-McKelvy residence could not more resemble a French chateau if it were in the Loire valley. It was, in fact, patterned after "Lalantré" at Versailles. The approach, with its parterre of matched trees together with exquisite formal gardens, completes the set. The simple entrance, framed under the segmental pediment, leads to a spacious stairhall; the formal dining room is on the right and kitchen and service quarters in the Mansard-capped wing.

Jacobethan Residences

140. Burke-Hanna-Wearsch House

Little Mountain Road, Kirtland
Authentic 16th Century English; Reconstructed 1924–25 by George Brown
Jacobethan

The story of this residence is one of the most unique in Ohio building. George Brown, an extraordinary Gates Mills stonemason, knowing of the existence of *an authentic* 16th century half-timbered house on the East Coast, communicated this knowledge to Edmund S. Burke, a wealthy Cleveland industrialist who was then developing an estate in the Chagrin Valley (County Line Road and Route 87) and prevailed upon him to buy it. It then fell to Brown, who had an apptitude for this kind of project, to piece the venerable structure together. Eventually (c. 1945), after Burke had moved to New York City, Leonard C. Hanna purchased the structure and again had it re-erected at his sumptuous estate on Little Mountain Road in Kirtland. It is, without doubt, the only authentic (even if enlarged and remodeled) Elizabethan house in the State. Front elevation is pictured.

141. Burke-Hanna-Wearsch House

Viewed From The Rear
Half-timbered effect represents the building method which prevailed to the mid-nineteenth century; spaces between the wooden structural members were filled with "wattle and daub." The leaded window panes and the multiple chimney pots are characteristic of the Elizabethan period.

142. Burke-Hanna-Wearsch House
Dining Room—Interior
Entire effect, including the panelled walls, beamed ceiling, and Tudor fireplace flanked by hand carved posts, is of the period of England's great Queen.

142A. Burke-Hanna-Wearsch House
Parlor (Great Hall)
Unfortunately, the stained rafters of the high "cathedral ceiling" do not register in this photo, but the character of the interior space, as currently furnished, is evident.

143. The Hermit Club   (*page 122*)
1629 Dodge Court, Cleveland
Frank Meade, Architect
Jacobethan
This bit of Old England exists in a downtown alley behind Euclid Avenue's Bulkley Building. Meade was one of the more accomplished members of the first generation of academically-trained architects to practice in Cleveland commencing in the 1890's. The corbelled, carved elements are particularly delightful. This type of enticing retreat is what is so lacking today in the sometime sterile re-development of our cities.

144. "Glamorgan"

Colonel W. H. Morgan Mansion (1904–05)
Alliance
Willard Hirsch, Architect (Cleveland)
Jacobethan

"Glamorgan" takes its name from the county in Wales whence the builder's father emigrated to America in 1865. Finding his way to Alliance by 1871, he founded the Morgan Engineering Company of which Colonel William Henry Morgan became President in 1897. A trainload of Vermont marble, noted for its self-cleansing properties, was imported for the building of Morgan's manor. Considering the rectangular windows with stone mullions and transoms, the prominent gable with bay, the building materials employed and other Tudor forms present, architect Hirsch built here one of the most faithful Jacobethan residences in Ohio. Before destruction by fire, the tower, containing exquisite hand carved woodwork, was illuminated by a sizeable skylight.

145. Van Sweringen House (1924)
17400 South Park Boulevard, Shaker
  Heights
Phillip L. Small, Architect
Jacobethan
Phillip L. Small was another of the more gifted designers to practice in Cleveland during the first half of the twentieth century. He and his firm were architects for the fabulous Van Sweringen Brothers who rose from orphaned beginnings to become builders of a great railroad and real estate empire. Solid, large and handsome inside and out, such a house in late 19th century England would have been dubbed "stockholder Tudor." Rooftop slates are graduated from very large at the eaves to small at the ridge to accentuate perspective. Small and his firm were also architects for the Van's "Daisy Hill Farm" in Hunting Valley east of Cleveland (Confer Figure No. 507).

146. Francis Drury Residence (1926–27)
Corner Cedar and S.O.M. Center Roads,
  Gates Mills
Charles Schneider, Architect
Jacobethan
Before designing this stone and half-timbered residence on the western slopes of the Chagrin Valley for Clevelander Francis Drury, Schneider had mastered the Tudor forms in executing "Stan Hywet" (Figure No. 155) for rubberman, Frank Seiberling of Akron—the house for which he is best known. For over two decades this former dwelling—now known as "Tudor House"—has served as the office, dining and social hall of Gilmour Academy.

148. Governor's Mansion (1925)
358 N. Parkview Dr.
Bexley (Columbus)
Jacobethan Revival
The present Governor's mansion was originally built for the Jeffrey family c. 1925. It would be a more convincing example of its style if the two-story bay in the gable at right were constructed of stone mullions and transoms. However, the native Ohio milled limestonework framing the vestibule interior, hall doorways and the fireplace is impressive. Hall and rooms are spacious.

149. House at 2730 Ridgeway Avenue
Oakwood (Dayton)
Jacobethan Revival

147. Francis Drury House (*page 125*)
Detailed—Gabled Entrance Porch, Chimney
Where gables intersect the roof, there are no copper valleys—the slate being continuous. Homes in this style are derived from the designs of English architects, Norman Shaw, James Webb and their followers. The multi-pot chimney is typical.

150. **Kulas-Levin Residence** (1932)
West Hill Drive. Gates Mills
Charles R. Greco (Boston), Architect
George B. Mayer, Resident Architect
Jacobethan

The lovely home which Charles Greco designed for steelman, Kulas, as the nation sank into the great depression of the 1930's has an old English quality without being a slavish copy of earlier precedents. Telltale forms are again the steeply pitched gable, the height of which exceeds the general roof line, and the prominent chimneys. The light colored stucco, perforated by stones here-and-there, adds a lightness to the composition complementary to the half-timbered effect so prominent in the rear elevation.

151. **Kulas-Levin Residence**
Rear Aspect
From this formal rear terrace one surveys a broad sweep of the Chagrin Valley.

152. Kulas-Levin Residence
Entrance Hall
The staircase is reminiscent of that in Ham House (1610), a notable Jacobethan manor on the outskirts of London.

153. Kulas-Levin Residence
Living Room
A manorial quality is imparted by the trussed beam ceiling with balcony and the perforated wooden screen permitting a vista from the far end of the "great hall' through the entrance hall.

154. Ford-Knight House (1927)
28523 E. River Road, Perrysburg
Mills, Rhine, Bellman, Nordhoff—Architects
Jacobethan
Among the many fine homes which line the Maumee River at Perrysburg is this originally built by Edward Ford of Libby-Owens-Ford Glass Corporation. Tudor forms evident are the squat-arched entrance, the bow window above with its leaded glass and the stone mullions and transoms of the ground floor windows. Half-timbered construction and rusticated, tile roof complete the picture.

157. "Stan Hywet"
Stair Hall
Staircase, ascending the tower of the great house, is reminiscent-in workmanship and design—of many in Elizabethan England.

155. "Stan Hywet" (1911–15)
North Portage Path, Akron
Charles Schneider, Architect
Jacobethan

When built for Frank Seiberling, President of The Goodyear Tire and Rubber Company, "Stan Hywet" was a "show place" and so it continues to be to this day—a generation after his death. Architect Schneider accompanied Seiberling to Europe early in 1911 to select a style for the great home the industrialist wished to build. The French Chateau mode was considered, but ultimately John Nash's Ockwell Hall and Compton Wynyates, a pair of Elizabethan manors, became the inspiration for this Ohio "transplant." Characteristically, red brick with contrasting stone window and door surrounds (architraves) were employed in its construction. Stone is also used for the window mullions and—in the multiple, tower window—for the transoms as well. Gables are steep; barge boards are decorated; chimneys are emphasized.

156. "Stan Hywet"
The Great Hall

Beyond a modest vestibule, the visitor enters a "great hall"—the beamed ceiling of which extends through the full height of the structure. Wood carvers were imported to execute the linen-fold, oak panelling of the minstrel's balcony, halls and other elements.

158. **Hillbrook Club** (c. 1924–25)
Route 87 at County Line Rd. Russell
  Twnshp.
Meade & Hamilton, Architects
Jacobethan
This impressive, half-timbered residence
was originally built as a summer "cottage"
on a 400 acre estate for Cleveland industrialist, Edmund S. Burke. The amazing
Burke-Hanna-Wearsch house (Cf. Fig.
140–142A), originally re-erected on this
property, served to accomodate Burke's
guests. The "cottage's" most interesting
room (Fig. 158A) is the downstairs library
whose woodwork, enhanced by a marvelous patina, is said to have been imported
from England. The hand of George Brown
of Gates Mills is evident in the masonry
walls enclosing the entrance courtyard and
garden elements.

Wrightian Homes in Ohio

159. Wescott House (1905)
1340 E. High Street, Springfield
Frank Lloyd Wright, Architect
Prairie Style
In 1905 Burton J. Wescott commissioned Wright to design the only authentic "Prairie Style" house in Ohio. Horizontality, low profile, banded windows, broad eaves and the early use of poured concrete are typical characteristics observed here. The large planters are a virtual signature of the renouned architect. Unfortunately this house, which ought to be one of Ohio's treasured landmarks, has suffered steady deterioration during recent years.

160. Ellis A. Feiman House (1954)
452 Santa Clara Road, Canton
Frank Lloyd Wright, Architect
Wrightian
Horizontality and the essentially flat roof with broad overhang are the most noteworthy features in the exterior design here. Usonian houses of this type are far less pretentious than the earlier Prairie School houses exemplified by Wright's Wescott House.

161. Ellis Fieman House
Living Room
The dining area in the background is balanced on the opposite wall by a sunken, corner fireplace and chimney laid up in neat brick "strata." Wall at right is lined with bookshelves with clerestory windows above. The principal entrance is at the right beyond which a corridor leads to the bedrooms.

162. Dobkins House (c. 1952)
5120 Plain Center Road No. Canton
Frank Lloyd Wright, Architect
Wrightian
The horizontality, so evident in this overall aspect, is emphasized at close range by the manner in which the buff brick is laid—all stretchers, no headers. Soaring shed roof and large glass expanse are design features making for a spacious parlor (left).

163. Lincoln Gries Residence (1968)
Fairlawn
Visnapuu & Gaede (Cleveland), Architect
Wrightian
The influence of Frank Lloyd Wright is
evident in this design by admirer, Robert
C. Gaede, who has here combined a low
profile with "striping," banded windows
and an idyllic situation.

164. Lincoln Gries House
Entrance Detail
Closeup of the entrance area illustrates the
fine detailing including an interesting ex-
tension of the overhang to accomodate the
extended bay. "Striping" is reflected in
the lantern.

165. Lincoln Gries Residence
Rear Elevation
Cantilevered sunroom, facing a dense woods, makes a fine perch for bird-watching and dreaming.

166. Lincoln Gries Residence
Sunroom
Aspect from rear sun deck through tile-paved front entrance hall. As in Wright's Feiman House (Figure No. 161), the exterior brick re-appears in the corner hearth and adjacent walls.

167. Stanley Meisel Residence (1964)
28849 South Woodland, Pepper Pike
William Morris, Architect
Modern
Frank Lloyd Wright's influence may be seen in this "glass house" but not pervasively enough to be truly "Wrightian." Morris has avoided the troublesome mitred glass corner windows.

Other Contemporary Homes

168. **Hale-Schaffner House** (1967)
Falls Road, Hunting Valley
William Morris, Architect
Modern
The Hale homestead is here viewed from the west bank of the Chagrin River adjacent to the Metropolitan Polo Field. It is supported by concrete posts in ready anticipation of high water. The interior space is interestingly arranged to provide exciting vistas of the sylvan scene.

169. **Willis Hale House**
Deck Area
The Hale house is, however, made for outdoor living. The substantial deck area exceeds its interior floor space

170. **Wayne Albers Residence** (1967)
Jackson Road, Moreland Hills
William Morris, Architect
Modern
Perched on a precipice formed by an abrupt turn in the West Branch of the Chagrin River, the towering Albers house is one of the most unique and exciting contemporary homes in Ohio. It is constructed of cedar. The living room extends through the full height of the two large windows of the facade shown—an impressive space when viewed, together with the woods beyond, from the split level dining balcony. The approach is, of course, from the backside where, upon entering, one is confronted with a choice of floor levels.

171. **Wayne Albers House**
Balcony dining area overlooks "studio" livingroom.

172. **Wayne Albers House**
The "studio livingroom.

173, 174. Walden Estates (1970–71)
Aurora-Hudson Rd.
Portage County
William Morris, Architect
Manuel Barenholz, Developer
Contemporary
"Country-Club estates," combining contemporary residential designs with leisure-time opportunities (golf links, swimming pool, dining club, etc.) in a rural setting within commuting distance to the City, are the latest development on the Ohio scene. Favorite building materials are western, rough-cut cedar side walls topped with a roof of cedar shingles. Unique at Walden are frame condominiums (illustrated) which are indistinguishable from nearby single residences.

175. Richard Fleischman House (1969)
1757 South Belvoir Boulevard,
Richard Fleischman, Architect
South Euclid
Contemporary
Architect Fleischman designed his own home around the basic philosophy that a house is made for its occupants and their fun. It is also built for vistas—to the outside and between focal points within. The exterior walls of rough-cut cedar siding enclose eight living levels.

176. Don Hisaka Residence (1968)
14300 Drexmore Road, Shaker Heights
Don Hisaka, Architect
Contemporary
Architect Hisaka's home was, in 1970, the first Cleveland residence ever to win the coveted American Institute of Architects' Honor Award for design. Three corner-connected modules, one for food preparation and dining; one for the studio living room; and a third for a den with bedrooms above join with the garage to enclose a private, inner patio onto which all rooms look out. The outer walls are constructed of stained, rough-cut cedar.

177. Don Hisaka Residence
Inner Patio
Cloister-like patio enclosed by the polygonal arrangement of living units.

178. Don Hisaka Residence
See-Through Living Room
"See-through" living room viewed from "cloister-patio." Its ceiling extends through the full height of the house.

179. John F. Lipaj Residence (1964)
12010 Glen Valley Drive, Brecksville
John F. Lipaj, Architect
Contemporary
Photo portrays the street-side approach to architect Lipaj's residence. The living rooms are oriented so as to look out upon a broad expanse of the Rocky River Valley.

180. John F. Lipaj Residence
Aspect From Southwest
Maximizing a unique situation, the architect has constructed a patio—and beyond it—a Japanese garden from which (left) the terrain precipitously falls off to the river valley below. Wide overhang shelters the upstairs living quarters from the western sun.

181. Carl Petersen Residence (1967)
Oberlin
Dickson & Dickson, Architects
Contemporary
A very unusual house for an Oberlin Professor and his family. The unpainted cedar siding contrasts with tan panels containing the window and door openings. There is a "Voyseyan" quality in the expanse of unperforated wall surface; the grouped rectangular windows and the completely plain gables.

182. Carl Petersen Residence
Living Room
Within the "Voyseyan" character persists in the attractively furnished living quarters enhanced by white walls and a particularly handsome limestone mantel. Living room ceiling extends through two full floors (ceiling evident is that of the balcony-corridor connecting front and rear upstairs rooms).

Public and Commercial Buildings

Federal and Greek Revival Monuments

201. First County Courthouse (1823)
Old Chester (Meigs County)
Abel Chase, Builder
Federal
Photo illustrates the buttressed facade of the oldest existing square, hipped-roof courthouse in Ohio—unwittingly vandalized by the Chester Grange. The bricked-in opening of a former first floor window can be discerned to the left of the simple Federal entranceway. The external buttressing of the facade impairs its original appearance.

200. Replica of Original Capitol of the State of Ohio (1800:1940)
(Office of Chillicothe Gazette)
Chillicothe
William Rutledge, Original Stonemason
Georgian
If there is one architectural mode which may be considered to be uniquely characteristic of Ohio's early decades, it is the square courthouse with hip roof, generally following the design of the State's first Capitol Building, which we see here in replica. Henry Howe's *Historical Collections of Ohio* shows, by illustration, that similar square structures once occupied the central locations in a large number of county seats. Of these, the only original extant examples are at Somerset in Perry County and at Old Chester. The author surmizes that the architectural source may have been the Governor's Mansion at Williamsburg, Virginia, where the heavily dormered roof is capped with a balustraded deck (absent here) from which the cupola springs.

202. Perry County Courthouse (1828–29)
Somerset   (*left*)
James Hampson, Designer/Builder
Federal
Obviously inspired by the statehouses which preceded it at Chillicothe, Zanesville and Columbus, but by this time the designer has introduced a typically Federal entranceway in place of the Georgian ensemble seen in Chillicothe's replica. The courtroom was on the main floor and the jail in the rear portion of this brick building which served as the Perry County Courthouse until the seat was moved to New Lexington (1857).

204. Brown County Courthouse (1849)
Georgetown
Hubbard Baker, Designer
Greek Revival
The pair of Doric columns, in antis, framing the recessed entrance is a principal stylistic feature of this early Greek Revival courthouse which dominates the square at Georgetown. It is doubted that the clock-bearing, topmost element of the tower was part of the original building.

203. Highland County Courthouse
    (c. 1834)
Hillsboro
Federal (Transitional)
The unitiated might mistakenly classify this imposing structure as being in the Greek mode. However, the arcading of the windows on the facade and of the side walls is foreign to the Greek vocabulary; as is also the hexagonal cupola. The second floor houses an impressive courtroom with a shallow, domical ceiling. Rear wings are later additions.

205. Capitol Building Of The State Of Ohio (1838-61)
Columbus
Henry Walter, et. al., Architects
Greek Revival

Comparatively few Ohioians appreciate the high regard in which their State Capitol is held by architectural historians. Unquestionably the most important architectural landmark in the State, it ranks with the nations's best efforts of the Greek Revival period. Henry Walter of Cincinnati won the $500 prize in the competition for its design (1838) followed in second and third places by Martin Thompson, an associate of New York's prestigious firm of Town & Davis, and Thomas Cole, the Hudson Valley landscape painter. Though Walter's plan won the prize, the final building plan was an "amalgam" in which Cole's ideas figured importantly. Construction got underway in 1838; however, the building was dogged with delays and a succession of architects (five in all) including ultimately (1856) the appointments of Thomas Ustick Walter (designer of the United States Capitol dome) and Richard Upjohn (Trinity Church—Wall Street) as consulting architects. Even Isaish Rogers (Astor Hotel, New York City, and Parker House, Boston) was called upon (1858) to design the steps, terraces and approaches as well as details of the interior finish-including the intricate tile floor under the rotunda. Despite the many delays and numerous architects, the design is quite as originally planned except for the deletion of the colonnade originally envisioned around the cupola. President Abraham Lincoln addressed the legislature in joint session here one month before assuming the presidency on February 13, 1861, and his mortal remains laid in state under the rotunda four years later following his assassination.

206. Ohio State Capitol Building
Inner surface of the shallow dome supported by a masonry drum 158 feet above ground level. At its center the Seal of Ohio is executed in art glass.

207. Ohio State Capitol Building
Senate Chamber

Although the building was commenced in 1839, interruptions delayed progress so that the legislative chambers were not completed until 1856. The Victorian influence is seen in their woodwork—especially the window surrounds. Thomas U. Walter and Richard Upjohn had been appointed supervisory architects earlier that year.

211. Ohio State Capitol Building
"Monument To The Great"

Monument on the Capitol grounds immortalizes the Generals who have brought honor to the Great State of Ohio.

208, 209. **Ohio State Capitol Building**
Hall of Representatives

210. **Ohio State Capitol Building** →
House Chamber Dais From Which Abraham Lincoln Spoke in 1861
Abraham Lincoln addressed the joint legislature meeting in this room in 1861 while en route to his inauguration in Washington. There was additional excitement on this occasion since the structure had just been completed. The Seal of the State of Ohio in bronze is affixed to the dais from which, over the years, Ohio's great have also addressed the legislature. Note that the carpet bears the outline of Ohio in its design.

213. **Montgomery County Courthouse**
Aspect From Southwest
A unique feature of the Dayton Courthouse is the insertion of a free-standing Ionic column in the segmental recess at each of the rear corners. The architect's idea was to convey the first impression of a portico at this end as well. Furthermore, the lost space was not required by the oval courtroom within.

212. Montgomery County Courthouse (1847–50)

Third Avenue at Main Street,
Dayton
Howard Daniels (Cincinnati), Architect
Greek Revival

The Greek design of Dayton's Courthouse, an Ohio landmark of the first rank, is owed to Horace Pease, an enlightened citizen whose knowledge of classic architecture derived from the copy of Stuart and Revett's *Antiquities of Athens* in his library. The resolution of the Greek peristyle, through the employment of Doric pilasters on all wall surfaces, save the east facade which is preceeded by the stunning portico, takes the same scheme as that adopted by Henry Walter for Ohio's Statehouse (Confer Figure No. 205). James Winchet, who had been imported from Switzerland to work on the locks of the Miami & Erie Canal, is credited with installing the corbelled, circular staircase which, by ascending the wall of an ante-room, provides access to the domed courtroom gallery. Under the present tin, roof-sheathing there is a solid, slab-stone roof.

214. Montgomery County Courthouse

Courtroom Interior
Behind the Greek forms of the facade architect Walter conceived this oval courtroom with its Roman, Pantheon-inspired, coffered-dome ceiling complete even to the oculus (covered). The accoustics are such that persons at opposite ends of the gallery could communicate in a whisper— an unforseen and questionable advantage.

215. Montgomery County Courthouse

Portico Detail
Locally quarried limestone, sometimes known as "Dayton Marble" was used in the construction of these massive columns as well as in the rest of the structure. The pair of original cast-iron lamps (only one seen here) at first burned whale oil.

216. Ross County Courthouse (1856)
Chillicothe
Hollins & Altenreith, Designers
Eclectic
Stylistically, the Ross County Courthouse is a most unusual building. It was built at a time when the Greek Revival was giving way to eclecticism. The architect obviously determined to take liberties with the Greek. In doing so, he has come up with something without precedent, but which, at the same time, is not entirely displeasing. Stripped of its lateral wings it could as well be a basilica as a courthouse.

218. Knox County Courthouse
Facade Detail
This photo of the upper facade of the Mt. Vernon Courthouse brings into closer range the delightful, pedimental design including mutules hung with guttae which, true to precedent, decorates the raking cornice—while tryglyphs accent the architrave.

217. Knox County Courthouse (1855)
Mt. Vernon
Daniel Clark, Architect
Greek Revival
The Knox County Courthouse is one of comparatively few temple-style, Greek courthouses extant in Ohio. Built during the waning years of the Classic Revival, it is contemporary with the deviant model at Chillicothe while following those at Dayton and Canfield by from five to ten years. The white trim contrasts effectively with its warm-toned brick fabric. The clock, added in 1901, in all probability pre-empted a more typically Greek second stage element in closer harmony with the tower base.

219. "Our House" Tavern (1819)
Gallipolis
Henry Cushing, Builder (Ohio State Memorial)
Federal
"Our House," a tavern, was erected to serve the busy passenger traffic moving along the Ohio River in pioneer days. It is now administered by the Ohio Historical Society which restored and appropriately furnished it in 1966. Built of brick, in Flemmish bond, it contains a taproom, public and private dining rooms, three bedrooms and a ballroom. The kitchen, according to local custom, occupied a separate little brick building (still extant) in the rear.

220. Morgan County Courthouse (1858, 1960)
McConnelsville
William P. Johnson, Architect
Eclectic
The McConnelsville Courthouse is a transitional building. Classic forms are still evident in its portico, pilastered sidewalls and pedimented cornice and portal. However, the roofline and the topmost tower element portend the Second Empire style.

221. Oliver House (1859)
Broadway at Ottawa, Toledo
Isaiah Rogers, Architect
Federal

Although built a generation after the Federal style had passed from the scene, the rounded bay upon which two lateral extensions converge (the site is triangular) and the semi-circular lights over the ground floor windows, are drawn from the Federal and not the Greek vocabularly. As originally planned, the Oliver House was to have had a prominent dome with cupola. Had these been executed the structure would display even greater adherence to the vestigal Federal mode. Isaiah Rogers was the most prominent designer of hotels in his day—having made his reputation with New York's Astor and Boston's Tremont House. In Ohio he also designed Cincinnati's Burnett House (with dome) which has long since passed from the scene.

222. The Golden Lamb Inn (1815)
Lebanon
Federal

The Golden Lamb was erected to serve travelers traversing the Old Post Road between Cincinnati and Dayton. Today, busier than ever, its dining rooms are a mecca known to most Ohioans. At least five United States Presidents and a host of other dignitaries have frequented its chambers. The bracketed cornice was most certainly a mid-19th century addition made in the course of an enlargement.

223, 224. Old Brick Tavern (c. 1845)
Route 40, Lafayette
Greek Revival
Parapet gable walls and Flemish bond suggest an even earlier date for this brick tavern which has served the increasing traffic along the National Pike for over a century and a quarter. The entranceway (detail in Figure No. 224), featuring overly slender Doric columns in antis, is the most pleasing element in the entire composition.

Italianate and Hi-Victorian Buildings

225. Fairfield County Courthouse (1871)
Lancaster
Blaire & Ebner, Stone Contractors
Italianate
In adopting a design for the second courthouse (pictured here) the Commissioners forsook the square, hip-roofed Georgian-Federal forms of the 1807 predecessor. Over-riding feature is the bold, bracketed cornice; however, careful inspection shows sophisticated stonework in the arched, window architraves and string courses which interconnect them.

226. Columbiana County Courthouse
  (1871)
Lisbon
H. E. Myer, Architect
Italianate
Less inspired (i.e., in comparison with the Lancaster Courthouse) is this model erected at Lisbon in the same year. Within a couple years the Mansard roof would make its appearance on the Ohio scene.

227. Delaware County Courthouse (1868)
Delaware
R. N. Jones, Architect
Italianate
The corbelled brickwork at eaves level suggests the Romanesque Revival; the bracketed eaves and roof-top belvedere suggest the Italian Villa; the window drip-mouldings, particularly at ground level, suggest the High Victorian Italianate. No matter, Italianate forms are everywhere in this early, post Civil-War deviant from Classicism.

228. Delaware County Courthouse
Telephoto lens captures workman checking the scales of "Justice" atop the cupola of the Delaware Courthouse. Similar idealized goddess' were ubiquitous courthouse adornments in this period.

230. IOOF Friendship Lodge (c. 1843)
Germantown
Eclectic
Not great, but a precious oddity on the
Ohio architectural scene. The base of the
structure (to the Gothic windows) is in
the Romano-Tuscan mode; the second
story is, of course, Gothic. Sign affirms
that the Lodge was organized in 1843.

229. Old Township Hall (1868)
On the Square, Sunbury
(Now Community Library)
Italianate
Originally built to house a school known
as the Sunbury Institute, Sunbury's Town
Hall has served a multitude of purposes
over the years. Today municipal offices
share the first floor with the County Library
which also occupies the second floor.
Fifty-five feet × thirty-five feet in dimen-
sion, it was built for the ridiculous cost,
measured by present day standards, of
$6,500.

231. Geauga County Courthouse (1869)
Chardon   (upper left)
Joseph Ireland, Architect
High-Victorian Italianate
Take away the rib-domed cupola, with
clocks affixed, and what remains is a
pretentious Italian villa. On the other
hand, the slim, lancet windows with trac-
ery and round heads suggest a church.
The picturesque courthouse occupies a
commanding position at the north end of
Chardon's "Public Square."

232. Athens County Courthouse (1880)
Athens   (upper right)
H. E. Myers (Cleveland), Architect
High-Victorian Italianate
In the Athens County Courthouse of 1880,
architect Myers has forsaken the Mansard
roof which characterized his earlier efforts
at Zanesville (1874) and Newark (1876)
(cf. Fig. 245). The pedimented entrance
pavillion, baroque dormers, ornate tower
and particularly the arched window treat-
ments are characteristic forms of the High-
Victorian Italianate style.

233. Kelley Block (c. 1869)
Milan
High-Victorian Italianate
The Kelley Block has long been considered
a splendid example of a mid-Victorian
commercial building. Aside from the visual interest of the bracketed cornice with
its segmental pediment and the window
hood mouldings, the principal interest of
the facade lies in the relatively early (Ohio)
use of a succession of slender cast iron
columns to support the subsidiary first
floor "cornice." Second Empire building
in the background is Milan's Townhall.

235. Amselm Holcomb Law Office (c.
1875)
23 Locust Street, Gallipolis
High-Victorian Gothic
The attorney who 100 years ago contracted
for this small office building located diagonally across the street from Gallia
County's Courthouse, has left to us the
handsomest structure of its type in Ohio.
The design is completely original. Note
how the decorative barge boards spring
from a pair of consoles centered above the
dual "arches."

234. Knights of Pithias Castle (c. 1885)
Jackson
High-Victorian
An exuberant piece of Victoriana in Jack-
son, center of an old iron-producing area
of the State.

236. Riverview Park Grandstand (1878)
Gallipolis
High-Victorian Gothic
This grandstand, quite probably executed by the same skilled carpenter retained by Anselm Holcomb to build his office, has come to be Gallipolis' trademark—even as The Soldiers and Sailors Monument is Cleveland's. The concrete walks approaching it were a recent gift of Gallipolitan Alden Howell.

237. Erie County Jail (1876)
Sandusky
High-Victorian/Eclectric
The banding and the polychrome effect obtained through the use of two kinds of stone, together with the abbreviated tower and carved eaves brackets, have caused us to make the above stylistic assignment of this eclectic building located on the south side of Courthouse Square. Its walls are said to be two feet thick. The structure, actually, looks more like some merchant's residence than a county goal.

238. Town Hall (1878)   ⟶
Mechanicsburg
High-Victorian Gothic
The most unique feature of this unique building is the novel use of cast iron columns in the corner niches—decoratively as well as functionally. There is a suggestion of banding, a Hi-Victorian Gothic device, in the stone string courses.

239. MacMillan's Book Shop (1873)
State Street, Salem
Victorian
MacMillan's Book Shop is Salem's oldest commercial landmark. Originally founded by Joel MacMillan in 1859 (a few feet east), it was moved to the present structure, built by MacMillan, in 1873. Its most noteworthy feature, from an architectural standpoint, is the use of cast-iron columns. The worn foundation stone strongly suggests relocation of the entrance.

Second Empire Buildings

241. Madison County Courthouse (1890)
London
G. Maetzel, Architect
Second Empire
Almost a decade later, architect Maetzel was called upon to do a courthouse at London which, considering its dual columniation and classic pediments portends the imminent Beaux Art Classicism. Still, the convex-sloped Mansard roof with its ubiquitous dormers and corner pavillions—hallmarks of the Second Empire style—predominate.

240. Allen County Courthouse (1882)
Lima
G. Maetzel, Architect
Second Empire
In searching out the cornerstones of Ohio's picturesque courthouses, one finds the names of the same architects recurring again and again. G. Maetzel contracted for at least three—in Allen, Shelby and Madison Counties—the first two of which appear to be virtual counterparts. Early American prototypes of the Second Empire style, which became so prevalent in Ohio during the late 1870's and 1880's were Boston's City Hall (1862–65); also Philadelphia's commenced in 1871.

242, 243. Wayne County Courthouse (1878)
Wooster
Thomas Boyd, Architect
Second Empire
Another architect, whose name is chiselled on several courthouse cornerstones, is that of Thomas Boyd, whose Wooster work is of particular interest for its sculptural detail. Hermes (Figure No. 243) support the corbelled pediment surmounting the principal entrance fronting on Wooster's "square." High above, on a split pediment, goddesses hold the ubiquitous scales of justice—symbolized in this instance, by the Ten Commandments.

244. Henry County Courthouse (1880)
Napoleon
D. W. Gibbs, Architect ←
Second Empire
Perhaps the most prolific of the Ohio courthouse architects was David W. Gibbs whose impressive Henry County effort, overlooking the Maumee River, is seen here reflecting the last sun rays of a July day. Again, justice, high on her perch, reigns over all—scales in hand. (Confer also Gibbs' work at Washington Courthouse, and Marion, Fig. No. 283).

247. Licking County Courthouse (1876)
Newark
H. E. Myers (Cleveland), Architect
Second Empire
In America the name, "General Grant," has also been applied to buildings in this style, but as Whiffen points out, this designation fails to take note of its French origin at the time of Napoleon III as exemplified by extensions to the Louvre Palace (1852–57).

245. Muskingum County Courthouse (1874)
Zanesville
H. E. Myers (Cleveland), Architect
Second Empire
The over-riding Mansard roof proclaims the style; however, the inter-connected window hood mouldings of the first and second floors are also hallmarks of the High-Victorian Italianate. The same fenestration is seen in Myers' Athens County Courthouse (1880) (Figure No. 232) by which time he had forsaken the Mansard.

246. Coshocton County Courthouse (1875)
Coshocton ↓
Carpenter & Williams (Meadville, Pa.), Architects
Second Empire
The rapid development of Ohio in the post-Civil War period, coupled with the explosive population increase and the inadequacy of the original hipped roof "square" courthouses and their Greek Revival successors, lead to a third generation of courthouses in the 1870's and '80's in which county vied with county, even as the Gothic cathedral-builders at Chartres, Bourges, Amiens and elsewhere had competed in the 12th Century.

Sullivanesque Buildings

248, 249, 250. People's Federal Savings & Loan (1917)
Sidney
Louis Sullivan (Chicago), Architect
Sullivanesque

The People's Savings Bank at Sidney, the best of the two Ohio commissions entertained by Chicago's great architect, compares most favorably with his small bank designs elsewhere. One immediately senses Sullivan's genius in the intricate geometric patterns carved both on the face and soffit of the great arch framing the colorful mosaic. Although now over half a century old, the interior, surfaced in smoothe-finished brick with oak trim, is as modern as tomorrow. Sullivan's other Ohio bank, in Newark, unfortunately does not retain its original facade.

251. **Spitzer Building** (1896)
520 Madison Avenue, Toledo
Bacon & Huber, Architects
Sullivanesque
Monumental, sculptured entrance suggests the work of Louis Sullivan but is not sufficiently geometric to be that of the master. Chicago window-bays and sophisticated masonry work about the windows confirms the hand of a competent designer schooled in the Chicago tradition. Offices on all four sides surround a central light well.

252. **The Allen Building** (Est. 1900)
Xenia (At Courthouse Square)
Sullivanesque
Although there is something of the Renaissance in the scale of the rectangular plan and the bold cornice, the organization of the fenestration within a series of arches extending from ground to cornice, is typically Sullivanesque. Without doubt the beauty of the structure has been seriously compromised by the modern, incongruous store fronts. Its fabric is red brick.

Richardsonian and Romanesque Revival Buildings

255. Greene County Courthouse (c. 1893)
Xenia
Samuel Hannaford, Architect
Romanesque Revival
Many of the forms observed in this architect's Cincinnati City Hall (Figure No. 421) are present here. However, the visual excitement conveyed by the latter's High-Victorian, two-tone effect is absent. Shades of Paris' St. Germain de Pres are seen in the tower and of the Chateauesque in the wall dormers.

253. Warder Free Library and Reading Room (1890)
Springfield
Shepley, Rutan & Coolidge, Architects (Boston)
Richardsonian
Shepley, Rutan & Coolidge were successors to the prestigious practice of Henry Hobson Richardson. In the Warder Library, as at the Asa Bushnell House (Figure No. 91), the Romanesque forms introduced by Richardson persist. The combination of light tan sandstone with russet stone, used decoratively, is most effective. The spacious, balconied reading room, with high, wooden trussed ceiling, was threatened (summer of 1970) by installation of an intermediate ceiling to form two floors.

256. Ottawa County Courthouse (1899)
Port Clinton
Wing & Mahurin (Fort Wayne), Architects
Romanesque Revival
Before the turn of the century, architectural firms tended to specialize. Readers have already seen how frequently the names of Hannaford, Myers, Gibbs and Maetzel occur as designers of Ohio's courthouses. Also concentrating in this area, Wing & Mahurin had just completed a similar courthouse at Greenfield, Indiana, in 1897.

254. Schmidlapp Free Library (1889)
Piqua
J. W. Yost—Probable Architect
Richardsonian
This facade is one of the delights that may be encountered when touring Ohio with architectural "antennae" attuned. After having "made-good" in the big city (Cincinnati), Mr. Schmidlapp ordered the former family residence reworked to fill the community's need for a public library. Arches on the first floor; lintels on the second floor—are equally powerful.

Second Renaissance Revival

257. Mahoning County Courthouse
(1908–10)
Youngstown
Owsley, Boucherle & Owsley, Architects
Second Renaissance Revival
Within the central pavillion there is an impressive rotunda illuminated by a partially glazed dome supported on pendentives; decorative murals on its soffit are by Edwin H. Blashfield. The attic inscription, above the colunnade, prophetically reads: "A Nation Cannot Outlive Justice. Where Law Ends; Tyranny Begins." A thorough modernization of the building was completed in 1963.

258. Mahoning County Courthouse
Illustrating the impressive central dome on pendentives.

259. **Clinton County Courthouse** (1916)
Wilmington
Werner & Adkins, Architects
Second Renaissance Revival
The Second Renaissance Revival between
1890 and the First World War was a
peculiarly American phenomena since, in
France and England, other directions were
being explored. Here the dome and the
round-headed window and door openings
at ground level suggest Roman rather than
Greek inspiration reflecting the fact that
the Renaissance was, in part, a rediscovery
of ancient Roman architecture. The photo
shows one of four almost symmetrical
facades.

260. **Washington County Courthouse**
(1901)
Marietta
*S. Hannaford & Sons, Architects (Cincin-
nati)*
Second Renaissance Revival
The rusticated ashlars on the ground floor,
also the arched door and window openings, hark back to the Renaissance. The
tower, too, suggests the campanile of a
Tuscan church or town hall. This structure
marks a switch for Hannaford from his
Richardsonian City Hall at Cincinnati
(Figure No. 421) and his Romanesque
Greene County Courthouse (Figure No.
255) both of which were completed almost
a decade earlier.

261. Auglaize County Courthouse (1893)
Wapakoneta
Kremer & Hart (Columbus), Architects
Second Renaissance Revival
Architects Kremer and Hart have here designed a more restrained expression of the Second Renaissance Revival than earlier efforts by Gibbs and others. The tall, octogonal drum, topped by a domical roof, with a clock on every other face, proclaims that it is indeed a courthouse. The main corridor, extending the length of the building, is decorated with panels depicting pioneer life by a German transient artist, Herr Dinkler (1928).

262. Warren County Courthouse (1895, 1835)
Lebanon
Second Renaissance Revival
Behind this facade of the 1890's, Lebanon's classic courthouse of 1835—considered then to be the finest in the State—still survives. The domed octogonal cupola, which takes its inspiration fron Renaissance sources, together with the female personification of Justice weighing her scales on the attic, identify the structure's function.

263. **Putnam County Courthouse** (1909–13)
Ottawa
Frank L. Packard, Architect
Ralph Snyder, Associate Architect
Second Renaissance Revival

The Ottawa Courthouse has been referred to as Beaux Arts in its style. To be sure coupled columns are one of that mode's most common forms. However, this is virtually the only Beaux Arts form present in a structure which basically belongs to the Second Renaissance Revival. It could well be the handsomest courthouse to have been built in Ohio in the first half of the 20th century.

266. **Dayton Art Institute**
Gallery Detail
Segmentally pedimented, tabernacle enframement of a second floor gallery exit; typical of the architectural detail embellishing this splendid structure.

264. Dayton Art Institute (1928–30)
Dayton
Edward B. Green, Architect (Buffalo)
Second Renaissance Revival
Along with Oberlin's Allen Memorial Art Museum (Figure No. 368), this museum would have to rank as the finest example of the Second Renaissance Revival in Ohio—nor is there a more impressive stair in Buckeyeland. As architect Green demonstrated that he was master of the Neo-Classic Style at Toledo (Figure No. 268), so here he displays his competence in form's deriving from Brunelleschi's Florence.

265. Cloister—Dayton Art Institute
Behind its well-proportioned facade is this cloister (one of two) within which one feels himself transported to Florence's Chiesa San Marco. The red tile shed-roof, below the corbel table, supported by slender stone columns, shades a peripheral ambulatory.

267. Butler Institute of American Art (1919)
Youngstown
McKim, Mead & White, Architects
Second Renaissance Revival
A comparatively rare Ohio work by the prestigious New York firm—the nearby memorial to President McKinley (Niles) being another of their commissions. The entranceway again suggests Brunelleschi's Foundling Hospital at Florence, Italy. A small, but lovely, formal Italian garden-terrace is enclosed by a pair of rear wings.

The Neo-Classic Revival

268, 269. **Toledo Museum of Art** (1912)
Monroe Avenue, Toledo
Green & Wicks (Buffalo), Architects
Neo-Classic Revival
After Cincinnati, Toledo's excellent Museum is the oldest, major art gallery in the State. It is the epitome of Neo-Classicism with its broad expanses of unbroken, wall surface and Greek ornament. Far wing (1924) is a later addition housing the famous glass collection. Exterior wall surfaces are faced with white Vermont marble.

271. **Rutherford B. Hayes Memorial Library** (1911, 1968)
Fremont
Howard & Merriam (Columbus), Architects
Neo-Classic Revival

This, the first of the Presidential libraries, was established to house the papers of the nation's 19th President. Since its founding the collection has been enlarged to cover many facets of American history and biography. Symmetrical, lateral wings (one of which is visible in our photo), designed by Hinkle & Paeth (Fremont) to accomodate the growing collection, were dedicated in October of 1968. The next Presidential library in this tradition is that of Franklin D. Roosevelt (c. 1945) at Hyde Park, New York. Since, those of Truman, Eisenhower, Kennedy and Johnson—each on a larger scale—have been established.

272. **Akron Art Institute** (1904)
East Market Street, Akron
Frank O. Weary (Akron), Architect
Neo-Classic Revival

This structure served for approximately 40 years as the Akron Public Library before being converted to Museum use. Beyond the vestibule, a spacious "well" extends through two floors—completely surrounded by a second floor "balcony." Architect Weary has come a long way since his Carroll County Courthouse (Figure No. 286).

270. **Farmer's & Savings Bank** (1906)
Loudonville
Neo-Classic Revival
A most impressive facade in an Ohio town having a population of 2,600. It is the only Classic element on an otherwise pedestrian Main Street.

Beaux Arts and Eclectic Buildings

276. Lake County Courthouse (1906–7)
Painsville
J. Milton Dyer (Cleveland), Architect
Beaux Arts
The Lake County Courthouse is one of two designed by competent Milton Dyer (the other—Summit) who, but half-a-dozen years earlier, had returned to Cleveland following five years at the L'Ecole des Beaux Arts in Paris. It is a comparatively simple and unpretentious building but the architect's Paris training comes through in the hefty central massing, the sculptural accounterments and the mini-monumental accents given to the entrance stair.

273. Lucas County Courthouse (1894)
Adams and Erie Streets, Toledo
Sidney Stine (Toledo), Architect
Beaux Arts
The dual columniation and central massing immediately place Toledo's symmetrical sandstone mass in the Beaux Arts style. It rises to a crescendo with the colonnaded drum and shallow dome, stop which stands a finial consisting of a squat column with an orb. The bronze McKinley Monument (foreground) was executed by Albert Meinart.

274. Miami County Courthouse (1885–88)
Troy
J. W. Yost (Columbus), Architect
Beaux Arts
Troy's Courthouse has often been called "the 'pride' of Miami County." We have earlier noted that architects seldom stopped with one courthouse. Yost here shows a considerable development in the few short years since his Guernsey County (Figure No. 282) effort. The raised pediment, the great central drum and dome together with the subsidiary domed corner attics, make something quite extraordinary of what would otherwise have been a "run-of-mine" Renaissance Revival model.

275. Miami County Courthouse
Facade Details
The "Pride of Miami County" viewed at close range.

279. Union Station (Entrance) (1897)
High Street, Columbus
Daniel H. Burnham, Architect (Chicago)
Beaux Arts
Now boarded and deserted—its very existence in jeopardy—still this impressive entrance to Union Station is a masterpiece, Beaux Arts composition from the base of its fluted columns to the acroteria. Designer Daniel H. Burnham, who but a few years earlier also designed the Wyandot Building at 21 West Broad Street, had been the "Architectural Titan" of the World's Columbian Exposition.

277. Tuscarawas County Courthouse (1882)
New Philadelphia
Thomas Boyd, Architect
Beaux Arts
Some historians might take issue with the stylistic assignment made for this structure. The building date is early for the appearance of a Beaux Art design in this remote provincial seat and the tell-tale dual columniation is absent. However, most other requisite forms of the style are present. Compare it with Boyd's Second Empire design executed only four years earlier at Wooster (Fig. 282).

278. Central Station Post Office (1911)
Madison Avenue, Toledo →
J. Knox Taylor, Supervisor—Architectural Office United States Treasury
Beaux Arts
Photo illustrates one of several entrances to Toledo's old Central Post Office—now in disuse. Dual columniation together with advancing and receding planes, both observed here, are hallmarks of the style. An American eagle maintains vigil from the pediment. Buildings of this type which sprung up all over the Nation at this time, were inspired by Chicago's World Columbian Exposition of 1893.

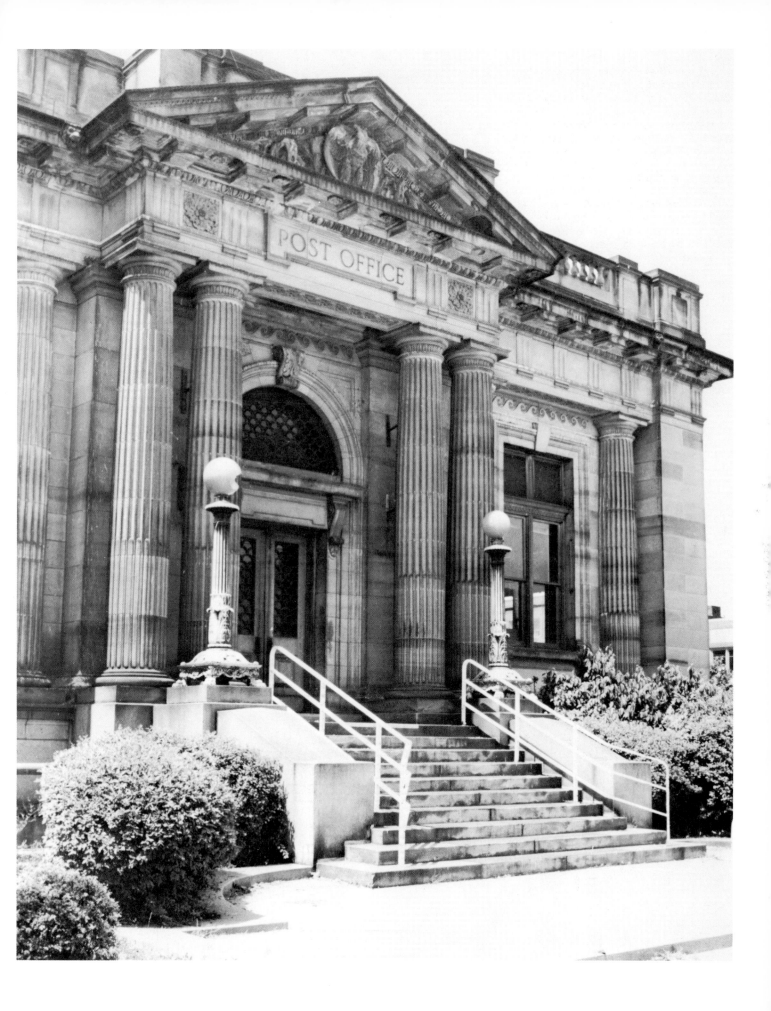

280. Dayton Daily News Building (1908)
4th and Ludlow, Dayton
Lester-Knowland, Architects
Beaux Arts
The highly sculptural character of this facade together with its almost complete fenestral penetration and Classic forms mark it as Beaux Arts. The visible "parade of columns," marches similarly down Fourth Street (unseen in photo).

281. Dayton Daily News Building
Portal Detail
Splendid, tabernacle entranceway to the Daily News Building. Superimposed "DN" in medallion above the door confirms that it never was a bank—as its pretension suggests.

282. Guernsey County Courthouse (1881)
Cambridge
J. W. Yost (Bellaire), Architect
Eclectic
The tower is a companion-piece for a Mansard roof; however, the architect has forsaken this over-worked form to anticipate the Second Renaissance Revival. Justice with her scales, as usual, occupies a plinth within the split pediment. The interior, as with many courthouses of this period, is quite undistinguished. Everything is known about the impressive Civil War Monument (dedicated June 9, 1903) except the identity of the designer—unfortunately an all-too-frequent circumstance in our land.

283. Marion County Courthouse (1884)
(Fayette County Courthouse) (1882–84)
D. W. Gibbs, Architect
Washington Courthouse
Eclectic
The stylistic assignment of this courthouse and its companion piece at Washington Courthouse is not an easy one. The round-headed window and door openings of the first floor dimly echo their counterparts in Florentine palaces; the second story pilasters and pedimented pavillons suggest earlier English adaptations of Renaissance forms. The bell-tower complex is, however, a purely American, High-Victorian invention. With this almost identical pair of courthouses both architect Gibbs and Ohio break from the ubiquitous Second Empire style for governmental edifices. (Murals by Archibald Willard decorate the first floor concourse at Washington Courthouse.)

284. Pickaway County Courthouse
(1888–90)
Circleville
Weary & Kremer, Architects
Eclectic
A most unorthodox design in which a turreted tower pre-empts a classic pediment. Another unusual note is the placement of a tabernacle-enframement around an arched entrance. The coursed ashlars are of an attractive rose-tinted sandstone while the trim is carried out with smoothe-finished limestone. (Frank Weary also did the Carrollton County Courthouse.)

285. Jefferson County Courthouse (1866–71; 1966)
Steubenville
Heard & Blythe, Architects
Hybrid Eclectic
A public building should at least "speak" honestly of its time. To convert a Mansard roof to modern, as the remodelling architect has done here, is to attempt to impose a new personality upon a mature individual. It will not work—and the person who essays it opens himself to ridicule!

286. Carroll County Courthouse (1885)
Carrollton
Frank O. Weary, Architect
Eclectic
Such were the architectural currents and cross-currents in 1885 that, weary of the Second Empire and other High-Victorian excesses, architect Weary did not know which way to turn in designing this courthouse; the result might as well have been a schoolhouse. Weary was also at least partially responsible for the interesting architectural abomination at Circleville (Figure No. 284). His best work appears to have been the Akron Museum of Art (Figure No. 272).

289. **Wyandot Building** (1897–98)
21 West Broad Street, Columbus →
Daniel Burnham & Associates, Architects
Commercial Style
The subject is a characteristic example of Burnham's work in Columbus. The Chicago windows and the neatly detailed cornice are the most obvious stylistic features. Burnaham's firm also designed Cleveland's Cuyahoga and Society National Bank Buildings. The former—though of lower profile—resembles this Columbus project.

287. **Office—Union Cemetery** (1892)
Steubenville
It is difficult to declare the proper stylistic "cubby-hole" in which to insert this interesting bit of cemetery architecture. Though it is all post and lintel—the spirit is Romanesque. The bell from Jefferson County's first courthouse hangs in its belfrey.

288. **The Craig Building** (c. 1900)
Cambridge
Eclectic
Formerly the Craig Department Store, this building still retains the name of its original owner-occupant. Elaborate corbelling and crenelation of the cornice combine with the tourelle to produce a picturesque design recalling a medieval fortress. The designer of the Civil War Monument, dedicated June 9, 1903, is unknown.

Commercial and Modernistic Buildings

290. **State Office Building** (1932)
65 S. Front Street, Columbus
Frank W. Bail; Henry Hake (Alfred A. Hahn, Consulting), Architects
Modernistic
A splendid design which has served the State well for almost four decades. Its crowning glory is the Ohio State Library located on the 11th Floor. Further along the Olentangy (at right) is the relatively new Ohio Bureau of Employment Services Bldg. (1963) competently designed by Toledo's Richards, Bauer & Moorhead with assists from Potter, Tyler, Martin & Roth; also Tully & Hobbs.

291. **Lincoln-Leveque Tower** (1924–25)
Broad & Front Streets, Columbus
C. Howard Crane (Detroit), Architect
Modernistic
Ohio's most obvious example of this de-
corated style is seen here from a reflecting pond adjacent to the Bureau of Employ-
ment Services Building. Originally con-
structed for the American Insurance
Union, the building was purchased by
John C. Lincoln and L. L. Leveque in 1945.

Contemporary Ohio Buildings

292. **Richland County Courthouse** (1967)
Mansfield
Thomas Zaugg & Associates, Architects
Contemporary (New Formalism)
This third (or fourth) generation courthouse at Mansfield, Ohio's newest, reflects the great change that has taken place in building design over the past generation. Odd that the architect should have resorted to a semblance of the paired eaves brackets—a form so characteristic of its Victorian precedents. The colonnade effect is continued around the building as a blind arcade.

293. **City Building** (1968)
40 West Main Street, Newark
Blum & Sweeney (Newark), Architects
Contemporary (Miesian)
Medium-sized Newark has reason to be proud of its new City Building which serves to impress visitor and resident, alike, with the progressive spirit of the community. The frank exposure of the concrete encased structural members, contrasting with the brick fabric, evidences Miesian influence.

294. Stark County Historical Society
  (1962–63)
749 Hazlett Avenue, Canton
Firestone & Motter, Architects
Contemporary (New Formalism)
The Stark County Historical Society appropriately nestles at the base of the monument honoring the memory of President William McKinley. Features of its design are five concrete barrel vaults, each 30 feet long and weighing 30 tons, supported by Indiana limestone columns 30 feet in height. The building contains a Planetarium in addition to the usual historical exhibits.

295. Stark County Historical Society
Lobby Interior indicating concrete barrel
  vaults.

296. Ohio State Historical Society (1970)
E. 17th Street at I-71, Columbus
Byron Ireland & Associates, Architects
Brutalist-Wrightian

This daring design is considered by some to be the most significant institutional building to be erected in Ohio since the State House (Confer Figure No. 205). The mass of its 196 foot square block is supported by cantilevers composed of prestressed, steel-reinforced concrete resting on four massive, hollow piers. Sixty thousand square feet of museum space (archeology, history, and natural history) is novelly arranged at or below ground level while the library-archives block (cantilevered) features a three-story, sky-lighted reading room. The architect was formerly associated with Eero Saarinen in the planning of St. Louis' great Gateway Arch and Museum.

297. Ohio Historical Society
A close-up view illustrating the powerful cantilever.

298. Football Hall of Fame (1963)
Canton
Cox & Forsyth (Canton), Architects
Contemporary (Miesian-Wrightian)
Miesian for the manner in which the roof is "hung" from external beams supported only at their extremities; Wrightian for its innovative form.

299. Christopher Inn (1963)
West Broad Street, Columbus
Karlsberger & Associates, Architects
Contemporary
Chicago's Marina City (1964) with which the Christopher Inn is contemporary, has inspired a rash of circular buildings around the country. Here, as at Chicago, the floors, divided into pie-shaped rooms, are cantilevered from the central core which houses elevators and utilities. A spiral, drive-in ramp encircles the lower three floors to provide parking space.

300. City National Bank Computer Center
(c. 1968)
Columbus
Brubaker & Brandt, Architects
Contemporary (Miesian-Wrightian)
A splendid illustration of the pride which the modern corporation takes in its plant. Not only is the architecture crisp, clean and functional, but aesthetics have not been overlooked. (Confer also Brubaker & Brandt's Beasley Convocation Center, Figure No. 389, at Ohio University).

301. Packard Music Hall (1954)
Warren
Contemporary
A portal known to millions of Ohioans within which the muses ploy.

302. Libbey-Owens-Ford Building and Plaza (1960)

Madison at Ontario, Toledo
Skidmore, Owings & Merrill (New York City), Architects
Contemporary (Miesian)

Toledo's Libbey-Owens-Ford Building is one of a comparatively few works by this noted firm in the State. Miesian influence is manifest. The aluminum studding, between the windows, extending continuously upwards from the second floor level, imparts a pleasing verticality. A principal design feature, however, is the "open space" (plaza) which the architects have created around three sides of the building "framing," as it were, the recessed glazed, ground floor enclosure fronting on Madison Avenue containing a spacious reception center.

303. Akron Public Library (1969)

North Main Street, Akron
Tuchman & Canute, Architects
Contemporary (Miesian)

Miesian concepts also strongly influenced the designers of Akron's splendid, new Main Library. The precise, geometric exterior gives little hint of the warm, colorful and light interior where, without wall partitions, space flows from one area to the next. The poured concrete inner wall surfaces offer the perfect foil for the many permanent sculpture, enameled panels and textile art forms by local artists which add to the visitor's pleasure.

303A, 303B. **Canton Art Institute** (1970)
Cleveland Ave.
Canton
*Lawrence, Dykes, Goodenberger & Bauer,
    Architects*
Contemporary
The principal entrance illustrated only
suggests the essential horizontality of this
marvelous gift of The Timken Foundation
to Canton's cultural life. Within the grand
foyer all eyes focus upon the cast aluminum "Pegasus" (Fig. 303b) by native son
Henry Mitchell—poised on the plinth from
which water spills to the pool beneath.
The structure combines galleries for the
display of art, a library and auditorium
facilities.

Some Noteworthy Ohio Churches

304. First United Presbyterian Church (1810–11)
West Union
Thomas Metcalf, Builder
Georgian-Vernacular
Our stylistic assignment is made largely on the basis of the Palladian motif in the squat tower. The porch is quite likely a later addition. The interior is most impressive. This is believed to be the oldest church in continuous use in Ohio.

305. Congregational Church (1822–25)
Tallmadge
Lemuel Porter, Master-Builder
Federal
Shortly after coming to Tallmadge from Waterbury, Connecticut, Porter was commissioned to do the joinery work on this unique Ohio church. It is not, therefore, surprising that he should have designed it along the lines of the contemporary Connecticut prototypes with which he was familiar. Consequently, the Tallmadge church would be quite as much at home in such Connecticut towns as Old Lyme or Litchfield as in Tallmadge, Ohio—perhaps more so considering the unbridled commercialism overtaking the once-lovely Tallmadge common.

307. **St. Lukes Episcopal Church** (1837)
Broadway, Granville
Benjamin Morgan, Architect/Builder
Greek Revival
The Episcopal Church with Doric columns, in antis, occupies the foreground. Behind it, and to the right in our photo, is the former Baptist Church of 1849 bearing a very proper Greek Revival tower consisting of box-like elements in receding stages. St. Lukes' antae and corner pilasters bear attractive fret-work taken from one or another of the numerous builder's guides then available. Morgan was also the builder of the nearby Avery-Downer House (Figure No. 46).

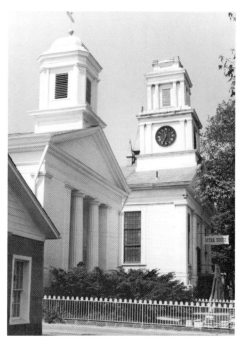

306. **Kirtland Temple** (1833–36)
Kirtland
Joseph Smith and Followers, Builders
Eclectic
Like the Gothic cathedrals of France, the Kirtland Temple was built with the combination of heavenly devotion, time and expertise contributed by every male member of the congregation. Stylistically, it melds the Federal and Gothic modes. The inner sanctuary consists of a central, vaulted "nave," with multiple pulpits at either end, flanked by side aisles. Unquestionably one of the most ambitious structures of its time in the Western Reserve; the wonder is that the Mormons deserted it within a year or two of its completion.

307A Christ Episcopal Church (1832, 1961)
Windsor Mills
Greco-Gothic
This little Ashtabula County Church is the epitome of dozens of modest meeting houses built in the earliest decades of the Western Reserve. Its pristine appearance reflects the reverence, the morality and the simple life-style of the pioneers from New England.

308. The Chapel (1836)
Western Reserve Academy, Hudson
Simeon Porter, Builder/Architect
Greek Revival
Simeon Porter and his father Lemuel, who passed away in 1830, were responsible for the design and construction of all the buildings which once comprised the "Monumental Brick Front" at Hudson. Of these the only original ones remaining today are the Chapel, the President's House, and the Atheneum. The Chapel, one of the most highly regarded Greek buildings in the State, underwent substantial alterations during the 1960's to shore up its failing walls and to insert two additional bays at the east end. The tower was originally heightened by an additional cubical element.

309. Atwater Congregational Church
   (1841)   (*upper left*)
Atwater
Greco-Gothic
The Atwater Church, like many others in
northeast Ohio, combines Classical and
Gothic forms. It was built at a time of a
revival in both styles; the Gothic, of course,
never lost its ecclesiastical connotation.
The tower cupola is a Victorian addition.

310. Universalist Church (1837)
Route No. 22, Montgomery (*upper right*)
James Jones, Builder
Greek Revival
Neatly contrived brick, Doric columns are
a principal feature of interest in this venerable Church on Cincinnati's outskirts.
The shingle covering of the pediment and
tower base are almost surely late additions
as is also the undersized and somewhat
ridiculous cupola.

311. First Congregational Church (1845)
Twinsburg Square, Twinsburg
Simeon Porter, Architect/Builder
Greek Revival
The Twinsburg Congregational Church is
the focal point of interest on the west side
of Twinsburg's Public Common. In designing the tower, Porter departed from
prescribed form, but perhaps his invention
is not too badly suited to an otherwise
orthodox Greek (Revival) temple.

312. St. Christopher's By-The-River
   (1853)
Gates Mills
Greek Revival
Scene of countless, fashionable weddings
in the quaint and exclusive Village of Gates
Mills,—facsimile of a small Connecticut
town. To its left a small park fronts on
the Chagrin River which flows serenely
behind. The sanctuary—in the building of
which Holsey Gates had a hand—was
restored by architect Frank Walker, circa
1930.

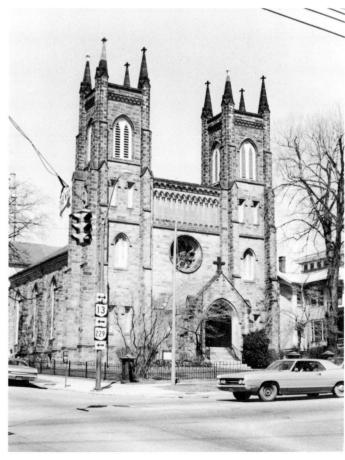

313. St. Paul's Episcopal Church (1841)
Maumee
Gothic Revival   ←
The brick for St. Paul's Church, one of
Ohio's earliest masonry, Gothic structures,
was ferried by rowboat across the Maumee
River from Thornton's brickyard in Per-
rysburg. Note that a row of "headers"
separates each four rows of "stretchers."
James Wolcott, whose home is pictured
in Figure No. 27, was the church's earliest
benefactor.

314. St. John's Episcopal Church (c. 1827)
Worthington   (*lower left*)
Gothic
St. John's would appear to be the earliest
Gothic church in the State. Cleveland's
namesake, St. John's Historic Church
(confer Figure No. 450), was built a decade
later to be followed by Maumee's St. Paul's
Episcopal in 1841. Like the nearby Orange
Johnson House (Figure No. 19), its bricks
are also laid in the Flemish bond. Finials
adorn the tower corners.

315. St. Paul's Episcopal Church (c. 1880)
(rest. 1967)
Mount Vernon   (*lower right*)
Gothic Revival
St. Paul's is typical of many churches of
its time scattered throughout Ohio. The
facade is perforated by an assortment of
window openings including: pointed
Gothic types of variable size, with hood
mouldings; narrow rectangular types with
Tudor label mouldings; and a central
round, rose window. An early parishioner,
Columbus Delano, helped nominate Abraham Lincoln as President and later served
as Secretary of the Interior under Grant.

316. Chapel (1872)
Baldwin-Wallace College, Berea
Gothic Revival
When built 100 years ago by hard working
German tradesmen, this first German
Methodist College in the United States was
known as German Wallace College. The
church, whose principal entrance we por-
tray, is constructed of sandstone from the
well-known, local Berea quarries.

317. **Quaker Meeting House** (1872)
Salem   →
Meeting House Architecture
A suitable house of worship for the Cistercians of the 19th century.

318. **First Congregational ("Two
    Horned") Church** (1906)

Marietta   (*lower left*)
Georgian Revival
Organized on the sixth day of December in the year, 1796, this Church may have valid claim to being the oldest religious body in the Northwest Territory. The earliest wooden structure (1809) on this site, facing the Muskingum River, also possessed square towers similarly flanking the pedimented facade of an essentially temple-style sanctuary, but in place of the pillared portico there was an enclosed shed-vestibule. Its first preacher was Dartmouth-trained David Story.

321. **Plymouth Church** (1924)
Coventry & Weymouth Roads, Shaker
   Heights   (*lower right*)
Charles Schneider, Architect
Georgian Revival
Here architect Schneider shows his mastery of the Georgian reportoire—even as he had earlier demonstrated the Jacobethan in Frank Seiberling's "Stan Hywet" (Figure No. 155) while simultaneously giving expression to a late revival of Classicism in the Motch House (Figure No. 117). The tower, screened by folliage, converts to an open, hexagonal belfrey topped by a flèche.

319. **Church of the Covenant** (1901
Euclid Avenue at 115th Street, Cleveland
Cram & Ferguson, Architects
Late Gothic Revival
A very early, solid example of the work of the Gothicist whose commissions ranged from New York's tremendous St. John the Devine to Pittsburgh's impressive East Liberty Presbyterian Church. The architect's Cleveland design recurs, in modified form, at Princeton, Glens Falls and elsewhere. The stained glass windows are notable.

320. St. Paul's Episcopal Church (1928–45)
Cleveland Heights
Walker & Weeks, Architects
(Byers Hays, Designer)
Late Gothic Revival
Trained at Carnegie Institute of Technology under Henry Hornboestl, Hays migrated to Cleveland and became one of the chief designing architects for the highly successful firm, Walker & Weeks. In addition to this work in the English perpendicular idiom, he played a leading part in designing Cleveland's massive Federal Reserve Bank, the Indianapolis War Memorial and later, in partnership with Ruth, spent seven years perfecting a contemporary addition (1959) to Cleveland's Neo-Classic Art Museum.

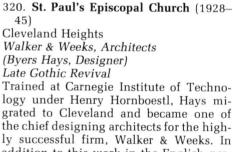

322. Temple Brith Emeth (1969)
Shaker Boulevard at Brainard, Pepper Pike
Edward Durrell Stone, Designer
Contemporary (New Formalism)
The periphery of this "temple-in-the-round" is mostly given to classrooms while the interior space is occupied, half by a sanctuary for religious services and half by a multi-purpose room, with their "stages" set back-to-back and separated only by moveable partitions, so that on special occasions the interior may be opened to form one huge space.

323. **Temple Brith Emeth**
Closeup of Peristyle and "Occulus"

324, 325. St. Stephen's Episcopal Church and University Center
Columbus
Brooks & Coddington, Architects
Contemporary
While the exterior is not displeasing, it is the interior of St. Stephen's which holds the greater interest. Its unobstructed nave is sheltered by a "cathedral ceiling" supported on a series of laminated trusses extending from floor to roof ridge. The brick chancel wall, illuminated from above, and decorated solely by a cruciform, is striking in its simplicity.

326. **St. Paul's Community Church** (1967)
Miami Road at Galbreath, Madiera (Cincinnati)
Contemporary
A contemporary church which the "builder watcher' cannot pass without a second look. The multi-faceted roof (foreground) shelters a hexagonal apse housing the choir. The walls are composed of alternate panels of stained glass and brick accented by vertical (white) structural members.

327. **First Congregational Church** (1931)
Broad Street, Columbus
John Russell Pope, Architect*
Gothic
This Columbus Church is believed to be the solitary work by the noted architect in the State. Although the windows are round-headed, the spirit and plan are totally Gothic. The interior provides seating in the nave which is separated from the ambulatory, side aisles by a series of broad, pointed masonry arches. The flambouyant, traceried rose-window is outstanding. The Church is of masonry construction throughout save for the roof. (*Assisted locally by Otto Eggars and Howard D. Smith).

328. Park Synagogue (1950)
3300 Mayfield Road, Cleveland Heights
Eric Mendelsohn, Architect
International
Park Synagogue is believed to be the only Ohio work by this internationally recognized architect. Its outstanding feature is the 100 foot diameter dome—claimed to be one of the very largest of its type in the world. It rests upon six reinforced concrete piers set in bed-rock. The dome, also constructed of reinforced concrete, tapers from a thickness of 8-1/2 inches at its base to less than 4 inches at the top—where it is capped by a "finial" bearing the Ten Commandments.

Other Churches included in this volume—

Cleveland

Cincinnati

Collegiate Architecture Past and Present

Antioch College

329. **Antioch Hall** (1852–53)
Antioch College, Yellow Springs
Alpheus Marshall Merrifield, Architect
Romanesque Revival
Merrifield here designed one of the State's outstanding specimens in the Romanesque Revival style. It is contemporary with James Renwick's Smithsonian Institute (1849) at Washington—perhaps the Nation's finest expression of this mode. Characteristic forms are the round-headed window and door openings, the twin pyramidal capped towers, and the extensive use of corbelled brickwork. Antioch Hall was remodelled in 1958 by an architect sensitive to its excellent initial design.

330. **Dormitory** on the Antioch campus illustrates both "lift slab" construction and the liberal, free-wheeling spirit for which the institution is noted.

331. Bowling Green State University Library (1967)
Bowling Green
Carl Bentz, State Architect
Contemporary
The striking Bowling Green State Library is surrounded by an elevated concrete terrace accessible either by a semi-circular pedestrian ramp or stairs. The principal stylistic features are the concrete panels at east and west ends, extending through the full height of the building, which carry an overall monochromatic design reminiscent of the Aztec-inspired mosaics which adorn the facade of the Library at the University of Mexico.

332. Bowling Green State University Library
Lobby Interior
Uninterrupted, the concrete "design-panel" (right) extends downward to penetrate the stairwell opposite the checkout desk, lobby and alumni lounge. It is illuminated by a sizeable skylight. Far end of the entrance lobby is given to exhibitions.

State University

333. Science Building (1970)
Bowling Green State University
Richards, Bauer & Moorhead (Toledo), Architects
Contemporary
Most recent addition to the exicting building program of the 1960's at Bowling Green State University. The fin-bearing semi-circular elements of cast concrete penetrate the entrance lobby creating a very novel effect within. The ground floor contains two demonstration "theatres."

334. Student Services Building (c. 1969)
Bowling Green State University
Sanborn, Steketee, Otis & Evans (Toledo), Architects
Circular Style
Photo portrays the low, circular profile of Bowling Green State's Student Services Building as seen from the Library terrace. A parallel might be drawn between the "Octogon Fad" of the 1850's and the Circular "Vogue" of the 1960's. This is Miesian architecture "in-the-round."

335. Student Services Building
Closeup
Closer aspect dramatizes the tapered cement supports and the ''amphitheatre'' approach to Bowling Green's Student Services Building.

Case-Western Reserve University

336. Harkness Chapel (1902)
Flora Stone Mather College
(Case-Western Reserve University)
Charles F. Schweinfurth
Gothic Revival (Late)
The grimey exterior walls, covered with the "fallout" of seven decades, give little portent of the impressive interior—essentially one large space whose roof is supported by great, wooden hammer beams. The Chapel was the gift of Cleveland's prominent Harkness and Severance families.

337. Clark Hall (1892)
Case-Western Reserve University, Cleveland
Richard Morris Hunt
University Circle
Queen Anne variant
Clark Hall, the first building to be erected by the College for Women (Flora Stone Mather) and Guilford Cottage, directly across the Green, were both dedicated in October of 1892. This is believed to be one of Richard Morris Hunt's rare—if not his only—work in the State. For its design he chose a gothiced variation of the Queen Anne Style so popular in that day. Its most striking space occupies the wing at right illuminated by the large, traceried window, where the "cathedral" ceiling is supported on massive hammer beams.

338. **Crawford Hall** (1969)
Case-Western Reserve University
Hoag, Wismar, Henderson Associates, Architects
Contemporary

Dramatic aspect of Crawford Hall, new home of the Jennings Computer Center on the campus of Case-Western Reserve University. It is constructed of precast concrete panels applied to a structural steel frame.

In the background is the Amasa Stone Chapel (1911) designed by Henry Vaughn of Boston—a Gothic companion piece to Cram & Ferguson's Church of the Covenant across the Avenue (Figure No. 319).

339, 340. **George Gund Hall** (1972)
Franklin T. Backus Law School, Case-Western Reserve University
Skidmore, Owings & Merrill, Architects (John Woodbridge, designer)
Contemporary
This newest addition to Case Western Reserve University consists of brick "oblong" and "round" elements joined by a second floor bridge. The former contains faculty offices and the law library; the latter, illustrated in Fig. 340, houses classrooms and a moot court. The bridge doubles as a lounge. The stunning structure replaces the Adelbert Rd. sandstone facility designed by Schweinfurth in the 1890's.

University of Cincinnati

341. McMicken Hall (1946)
University of Cincinnati
Hake & Hake, Architects
Georgian Revival

⟵

In designing this central unit of the University's "Monumental Row" fronting on Clifton Avenue, the architects reached back to the Georgian designs of our Colonial period which, in turn, were inspired by the English prototypes of James Gibbs (St. Martin's—London) and the builder's guides of Batty Langley, among others.

343. Enginering and Science Center (1970)
University of Cincinnati
A. M. Kinney & Associates, Architects/Engineers
Contemporary

A building so modern that it defies classification. Whiffen* employs the term "Brutalism" to describe this type of "flesh and bones architecture," favoring cast concrete construction, where deeply recessed windows perforate the solid walls of the rectangular form. (*American Architecture Since 1780).

342. The Van Wormer Library (1899)
University of Cincinnati
Samuel Hannaford & Sons, Architects
Neo-Classic Revival

It has been pointed out that there is no counterpart in the architecture of Europe for the Neo-Classic Revival which overtook the United States commencing in the 1890's. For this American aberation, we can thank Chicago's World Columbian Exposition of 1893 where the architectural commission headed by Daniel Burnham once again turned back to Classic forms for its inspiration. These are reflected in the Van Wormer Library (Greek Ionic columns; trabeated entrance).

Denison University

344. Swasey Chapel (1924)
Denison University, Granville
Arnold Brunner, Architect
Georgian Revival
Swasey Chapel was the gift of Ambrose Swasey of Cleveland. No doubt Mr. Swasey knew Arnold Brunner as the architect of Cleveland's Renaissance Revival Post Office and Custom House (1911) at the east end of Public Square. Here he shows his ability to design in the Georgian Revival style. The President's house (1902) in the foreground is also a Georgian Revival design.

345. Slayter Hall (1962)
Denison University, Granville
Joseph Baker & Associates (Newark), Architects
Meisian
A formal, precise, modular design by the competent Ohio firm which subsequently executed the Newark City Hall, and Marietta's spectacular, valley-bridging High School. Slayter Hall serves as the Student Union building.

Heidelberg
College

347. Beeghley Library (1967)
Heidelberg College, Tiffin
*Richards, Bauer & Moorhead, Architects
 (Toledo)*
Circular Style
This library "in-the-round" is one of the truly exciting architectural spaces in Ohio. As is so often the case on the state's campuses, it exists in juxtaposition to venerable College Hall (1886)—contrasting the new with the old. The building is arresting at any time, but it is particularly impressive at night when the spaced concave cement panels which surround the upper level are illuminated.

348. Beeghley Library
Closeup of the exterior revealing the architectural detail and the tubular columns which support it.

349. Beeghley Library
Interior
The excitement of Beeghley Library fully registers upon entering the lobby area where the central light-well with its curvilinear staircase, connecting ground and upper floors, comes fully into view. Open stacks are arranged like radii of a circle in surroundings which would entice even the most apathetic student.

346. College Hall (1886)   *(page 225)*
Heidelber College, Tiffin
Peters and Burns (Dayton), Architects
Eclectic
An eclectic building which, although built at a time when the Richardsonian Romanesque was sweeping the country, more nearly resembles the earlier Romanesque Revival style. Chamberlain & King of Tiffin contracted to build College Hall for $46,-558, however the ultimate finished cost approximated $60,000—a splendid value by 1972 standards.

Hiram College

352A **Bonney Castle**—Hiram College
  (c1848, 1972)
Hiram
Greek Revival
It would appear that, at some point after its construction, an additional third floor living-space was added to Bonney Castle. An appended front porch, removed in the 1971 restoration, no longer conceals the outstanding Classic entranceway. The structure, with associations going back to the origins of Hiram College, now serves as the English faculty center.

350. **Hinsdale Hall** (1867, 1886)
Hiram College, Hiram
J. N. Skinner, Architect
Eclectic
Hinsdale Hall is one of a very few non-existent buildings pictured in this volume. It was demolished in 1968 in a major campus re-development shortly after the photo was taken. As originally built, Hinsdale Hall had only two floors. Its former style was, however, completely lost in the 1886 remodelling when the tower and third floor were added.

351. The Kennedy Center (1969)
Hiram College, Hiram
Hunter, Howard & Saxon (Warren), Architects
Georgian Revival

Hiram's campus, too, "exploded" with new building during the decade of the '60's. For the new Kennedy Student Center, located on the former site of the venerable Squire House, the stately forms of the Georgian Colonial style were re-discovered. The building contains dining facilities, bookstore, lounges and offices for student activities.

352. Hinsdale Hall (New)
Humanities and Social Science Building (1969)
Hiram College
The Austin Company, Architects/ Builders
Miesian

The contrast between the new and the old Hinsdale Halls dramatically illustrates the revolution which has taken place in both building style and materials over the past century—perhaps the most striking advance of any similar period in human history. Miesian influence is evident in the frank expression of the structural framing. A commodious passageway, covered by a bridge, separates near and far "wings."

Kent State University

353A. College of Business Administration (1972)
Kent State University, Kent
Damon, Worley, Cady & Kirk, Architects
A handsome addition to the Kent State campus housing faculty offices, classrooms and an auditorium by the designers of the equally exciting Willoughby Fine Arts Center. A major innovation are the fan shaped classrooms with desks only five, segmental rows deep.

353. Taylor Hall (1968)
Kent State University
Ward & Schneider, Architects
Meisian
Taylor Hall, around which the tragic riots in the Spring of 1970 took place, houses the Schools of Architecture and Journalism. It occupies a height on the enlarged campus like a present day Parthenon and is easily the most prominent and impressive building at Kent. Cor-Ten sculpture to the left of light post is by Akron's Don Drum.

Kenyon College

354. Rosse Hall (1829–45)
Kenyon College, Gambier
Charles Prczriminski, Architect
Greek Revival
An architectural oddity on a campus which was largely Gothic until recent decades. Named after a benefactor, the Countess Dowager of Rosse, the structure served as the original chapel and assembly hall for many years. The interior space is uninterrupted.

355. Bexley Hall (1839–43)
Kenyon College, Gambier
Henry Roberts (English Architect)
Tudor-Gothic Revival
In 1836 when the competition for the design of the burned-out Parliament buildings was announced in London, two styles were specified—the traditional English architecture of the Elizabethan Period or the Gothic. We all know that the perpendicular Gothic won out, but had the scale tilted the other way, the Parliament buildings might have resembled Kenyon's Bexley Hall with which they are contemporary. The architecture of Bexley is derived from the medieval forms of structures such as Hampton Court Palace. It was, indeed, a remarkable building for its time in Ohio.

356. "Old Kenyon" Hall (1828–36)
Kenyon College, Gambier
Rev. Norman Nash/Philander Chase, Architects
Gothic Revival

"Old Kenyon" claims to be the oldest Gothic Revival collegiate building in America. The plans are Nash's; Chase supervised the building. There are no Gothic arches or crenelations here; the principle Gothic features being the pinacles. For some years the design of the entire building was attributed to Boston's Charles Bulfinch; however, it is now known that he only suggested the steeple's form. "Old Kenyon" burned to the ground in 1949, but has been reconstructed to exactly duplicate the original building in appearance.

357. Church of the Holy Spirit (1869–71)
Kenyon College, Gambier
Gordon M. Lloyd (Detroit), Architect
Victorian Gothic

In many respects, but particularly in the configuration of the spire, this Kenyon church resembles architect Richard Upjohn's St. Mary's (1846–48) at Burlington, New Jersey—a typical product of the early Gothic Revival. The banding of the roof is, however, characteristic of the High-Victorian Gothic period in which it was built. The interior is impressive.

358. Ransom Hall (1910)
Kenyon College, Gambier
Charles F. Schweinfurth, Architect
Jacobethan
In one of his comparatively few commissions outside of Cleveland, Charles Schweinfurth here designed, in the most compatible surroundings, a very convincing specimen of the Jacobethan Revival. A characteristic of the style, which the architect has here employed very effectively, is the interplay between the rusticated stone used for the fabric of the building and the dressed limestone of which the window framing and mullions are constructed.

360. Bushnell Hall (1965)
Kenyon College, Gambier
Vincent G. Kling & Associates (Philadelphia), Architects
Contemporary
These contemporary dormitories at "Old Kenyon's" rear, are another credit to the designer of Marietta's Fine Arts Center. (Cf. Fig. 362)

359. Ransom Hall →
Lounge
The lounge, at the center-rear of Ransom Hall, is a truly impressive recreation of a great Jacobean Hall in miniature. Here, true to form, the large windows are broken by stone transoms and mullions. The heavy hammer beam ceiling completes the architectural ensemble. Ransom Hall was originally built as an alumni library.

Marietta College

361A. **Mills House** (c. 1822)
Fifth and Putnam Sts. Marietta
Federal
This most impressive home, built by Henry P. Wilcox 35 years after the founding of Ohio's first community, is owned by Marietta College and serves as the abode of her President.

361. **Erwin Hall** (1845–50)
Marietta College, Marietta
Rufus E. Harte, Probable Architect
Greek Revival
As Professor Eric Johannesen has pointed out (cf. bibliography), this early Marietta College building strongly resembles The Chapel at Western Reserve Academy in Hudson (Confer Figure No. 308). The subject of our present attention is, however, more truly Greek since the prominent entablature, executed in brick, is carried completely around and omits the incongruous arcading of the side walls—a stylistic feature of the Hudson structure. When originally built Erwin Hall contained the Chapel and recitation rooms.

362. **Grover Herman Fine Arts Center** (1965)
Marietta College
Vincent G. Kling & Associates (Philadelphia), Architects
New Formalism

The Grover Herman Fine Arts Center is, for the author, one of the most aesthetically satisfying contemporary buildings in the State. The arcaded loggia is the modern counterpart of Brunelleschi's Foundling Hospital in Florence while the terne-plate attic is a Mansard derivative. The Center houses the College's art, drama and music departments. The ground floor contains a theatre for the performing arts preceeded by a glass enclosed lobby also utilized in the display of student art.

363. **Andrew V. Thomas Memorial Hall** (c. 1969)
Marietta College
Eesley, Lee & Vargo, Architects (Marietta)
New Formalism

The number of fine new facilities for higher education built in Ohio in the 1960's is nothing short of amazing. The design of this modern "Parthenon" with its clean, crisp lines will, we strongly suspect, stand the test of time when judged from the vantage point of 2070 A.D. It is utlized in the study of economics, business administration and by the Evening Division.

Miami University

364. President's House (c. 1837)
321 East High Street Oxford
(Remodelled 1966 by Cellarius & Hilmer)
Greek Revival
A comparatively unusual, brick, hip-roof Greek Revival house for Ohio. Unquestionably, the porch is a late 19th century addition. Its most prominent Grecian feature is the frontpiece design.

365. Administration Building (1956)
Miami University, Oxford
Cellarius & Hilmer (Cincinnati), Architects
Georgian Revival
The pedimented portico supported by four free standing columns is the focal point of interest in this mid-twentieth century reinterpretation of the Georgian style.

367. **Assembly Hall**
Vista down a section of the broad, circumferential entrance lobby.

366. **Assembly Building** (c. 1966; 1968)
Miami University, Oxford
Carl Bentz, State Architect, in association with James E. Allan
Miesian
Assembly Hall serves both as a place of convocation and as an indoor gymnasium. The area within is surrounded by commodious corridors providing access, by means of cantilevered stairs, to the stands above. The building and the space which it encloses are on a grand scale.

Oberlin College

368. Allen Memorial Art Museum (1917)
Oberlin College, Oberlin
Cass Gilbert, Architect
Second Renaissance Revival
Ohio-born Cass Gilbert, designer of New
York's famed Woolworth Building and one
of the Nation's more famous architects,
was called upon by Oberlin to design this
splendid representation of the Second
Renaissance Revival. The arcaded loggia
is the most prominent feature of the style
seen here, but the entire vocabulary is
present. Gilbert executed both the Detroit
and St. Louis Public Libraries in a similar
mode. The detailing is exquisitely han-
dled.

369. **Sophronia Brooks Hall Auditorium**
(1953)   (*page 238, top*)
Oberlin College
Wallace Harrison, Architect
Wrightian
Although not extreme today, when built almost twenty years ago, the Sophronia Brooks Hall Auditorium was quite "far out." Consider also the contrast between it and the Renaissance Allen Memorial Art Museum from which it is separated only by a small park.

370. **Bibbins Hall** (c. 1968)
Oberlin Conservatory of Music
Minoru Yamasaki, Architect
New Formalism
Bibbins Hall is the northern-most element in a three-unit, "U" design housing Oberlin's highly reputed Music Conservatory. Closed passageway (center background) connects it with Roberts Hall (at "U's" base) and the Warner Concert Hall. The uniquely fenestrated wallfacing is composed of precast concrete panels.

371. **King Memorial Hall** (1966)
Oberlin College
Minoru Yamasaki, Architect
New Formalism
Another example of Yamasaki's innovative work on the Oberlin campus diagonally across from the Conservatory. Visual interest is greatly enhanced by the contemporary Gothic "sun shades."

Ohio State University

372. **University Hall** (1873, 1896)
Ohio State University, Columbus
Original Designer—Synder (Akron)
Yost & Packard—1896 Remodelling
Second Empire
There is much that is Romanesque about
this original building of the Ohio State
University, however the Mansard roof with
curbing is the hallmark of the Second
Empire style. The survival of this major
physical link of the University with its
origin seemed threatened with destruction
in 1970, but it is hoped that the good sense
will be found to preserve it and bring its
interior space up to 20th century standards. (Note. University Hall was demolished in the summer of 1971)

373. Orton Hall (1893)
Ohio State University, Columbus
Yost & Packard, Architects
Richardsonian
This massive arch with its receding orders supported by columns with intricately carved impost blocks (also the rusticated masonry employed throughout) echoes the designs of Henry Hobson Richardson in Boston, Easton, Albany and elsewhere. The Hall has long been the home of the University's Geology department. It is the major Richardsonian building on a campus which incorporates many subsequent styles.

373A. Lovely, conically capped tower of Orton Hall viewed from the paved terrace before Mendenhall Laboratory.

374. William Oxley Thompson Library (1911)
Ohio State University
Allen & Collins, Architects (1950 addition—Howard D. Smith)
Neo-Classic Revival
The columinated facade of the Ohio State Library, preceded by a shaded plaza honoring former President William Oxley Thompson (1899–1925) faces the vast campus green.

376. **Drake Union** (1972)
Olentangy River Ohio State University
Tibbals, Crumley, & Munson (Columbus)
arch'ts—
(in association with Hollie W. Shupe OSU
Arch't)
Contemporary
This second "Union" on the Ohio State campus combines a Stadium Theatre for the performing arts with lounges, dining facilities and a boat house. The interior is attractively and colorfully furnished. High-rise building to the rear is one of the pair of Olentangy dormitories to which it is connected by above-street-level ramps. The building maintains a low profile.

379. **Stadium** (1920–22)
Ohio State University
Howard D. Smith, Architect
With the exception of Cincinnati's new river-front and Cleveland' lakefront stadiums, this is Ohio's greatest. Now, half a century old, it has doubtless served as a model for many other sports arenas about the country. If stones could speak, what stories these could tell!

375. **Brown Hall** (1903)
Ohio State University (Architecture)
Neo-Classic Revival
The Neo-Classic Revival is again obvious on the Ohio State campus in the portico and brick pilasters seen here. Note the neat handling of the brick work in the corbel table and window surrounds.

377. **Mershon Auditorium** (1954)
Ohio State University
Howard D. Smith, Architect
Contemporary

It neither belongs to the Miesian, the New Formalism, Wrightian or neo-expressionistic styles; therefore, let us cast it as a piece of "Brutalism" ahead of its time. For even if it is made of Indiana limestone, rather than poured concrete, it is rectangular and it is weighty and only on the near side is it perforated by windows. Viewed between the piers of the 15th Street Gate, it is an impressive, unencumbered work which, stylistically, will stand the test of time.

378. **Olentangy Dormitories** (1969)
Ohio State University
Schooley, Cornelius & Schooley (Columbus), Architects
Contemporary

The Olentangy dormitories, consisting of two 24-story structures, each with space for almost 2,000 students, constitute a new concept in university living in that they are co-educational and include under one roof facilities for living, dining and cultural development. They are located on a newly re-developed portion of the campus landscaped by James H. Bassett and connect directly with the new Drake Union by means of pedestrian ramps.

Ohio Wesleyan University

381. **L. A. Beeghly Library** (c 1965)
Ohio Wesleyan Univ. Delaware
C. Curtiss Inscho & Assoc., Architects
Contemporary
Openness of plan and ready accessibility
to the stacks are design features of Ohio
Wesleyan's new library which takes its
place with equally exciting facilities at
Ohio University, Heidelberg, Bowling
Green and Cleveland State.

380. Elliott Hall (c. 1833)   ←
Ohio Wesleyan University, Delaware
Federal/Greek (Transitional)
Originally a hotel serving the needs of
visitors to a local spa, Elliott Hall was
purchased with the founding of the college. The exterior design, marked by arcaded windows at the ground level and
pilasters extending through two floors, is
reminiscent of Bulfinch's Harrison Gray
Otis House of 1800 in Boston. It was
obviously designed and built by a competent master-builder whose identity is unknown. Authorities at the College liked the
design of Elliott Hall so well that architect
Morris Cadwallader was charged to closely
emulate it when Sturgis Hall was erected
in 1855.

382. University Hall (1891–93)
Ohio Wesleyan University
J. W. Yost, Architect
Romanesque Revival
University Hall stands on the site formerly
occupied by Elliott. The tower, accented
at its corners by rounded turrets with
conical caps, is the principal campus
landmark. The building is also known as
"Gray's Chapel".

383. University Hall
Detail
Broad semi-circular arch at side entrance.
The front entrance is quite similar.

384. Slocum Library (Est. 1898)
Ohio Wesleyan University
Renaissance Revival
The Roman Doric portico is the focal point
of architectural interest at the Charles
Elihu Slocum Library now superceded by
Beeghley Library.

Ohio University

385. **Manasseh Cutler Hall** (1816)
Ohio University, Athens
Benjamin Corp, Designer
Federal
Illustrated is the north facade of Ohio's
oldest collegiate building which, today, is
separated by formal gardens, at its rear,
from the new (1969) Vernon Alden Library (Figure No. 387). The south facade
is much the same except for a simpler
statement of the entrance and deletion of
the "compressed" Palladian window at
the second floor level. The interior was
remodelled in 1881–82 and again in 1946.

385A. Cutler Hall cupola detail.

386. **Galbreath Memorial Chapel** (1957)
Ohio University   (*page 247*)
Georgian Revival
Anyone familiar with All Soul's Church
(1824) by John Nash at the head of Regent
Street in London will know the inspiration for this tower.

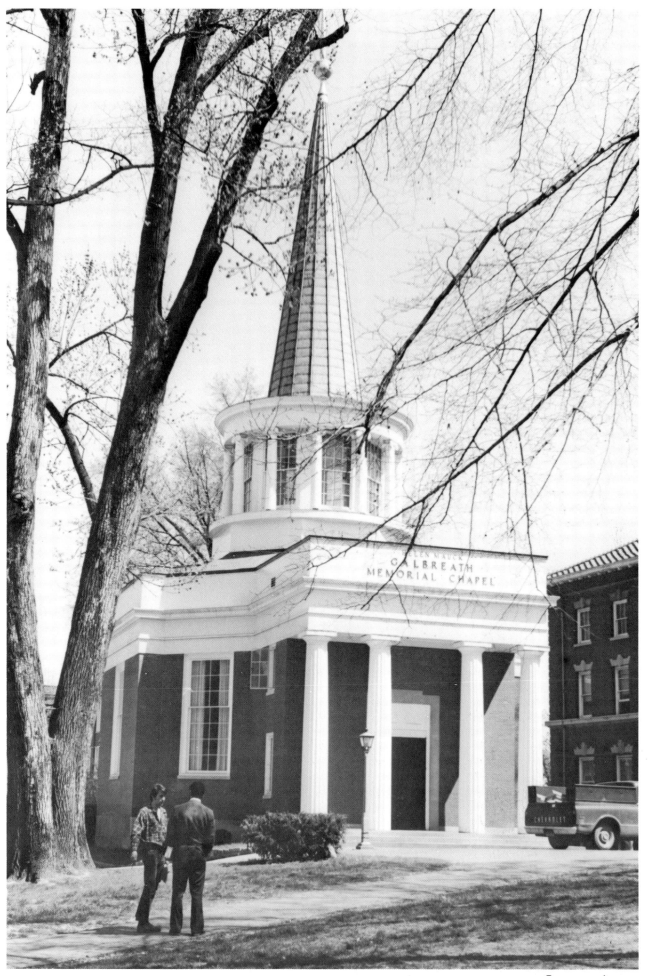

387. Vernon Alden Library (1969)
Ohio University
Dalton & Dalton (Cleveland), Architects
Contemporary
The new Vernon Alden Library, described
by its designers as being in a "formal"
style, is constructed of brick and cast concrete. Large window-wall sections of the
upper two floors containing the stacks are
integral, precast concrete panels.

388. Vernon Alden Library
Aspect from the street side illustrating the
modular construction.

248   COLLEGIATE ARCHITECTURE

389. **Beasley Convocation Center** (1968)
Ohio University
Brubaker & Brandt (Columbus), Architects
Circular Mode
Largest of the contemporary circular buildings in Ohio, Beasley Hall is essentially a great sports arena seating 8,000 or more persons. ("River" in foreground was relocated to clear the building site.) Unlike Beeghley Library or Bowling Green's Student Services Center—other collegiate "rounds" featured in this volume—Beasley is crowned by a squat dome. The "peristyle" of supporting columns suggest that the structure might be thought of as a circular expression of the New Formalist style.

390. **Beasley Convocation Center**
Lobby Interior
An inner access corridor surrounds the building. Enlargement of same opposite a principal entrance is known as "Ohio Athletic Hall" where the University's star performers are honored. Over all a "Bobcat" prevails. The building is a triumph of modern engineering.

Wooster

391. Kauke Hall (1901–02)
Wooster College, Wooster
Lansing C. Holden, Architect (New York City)
Jacobethan
Were there a drawbridge before the central tower, decorated with shield-bearing lions, one might imagine, when passing through this Tudor archway, that he was entering the outer court of England's Hampton Court Palace. The hall houses instructional facilities for the liberal arts. Its architect was a brother to the President of the college at the time Kauke Hall was erected.

392. Kauke Hall
Central Tower Element

College

393. Andrews Library (1962)
Wooster College
Schafer-Flynn & Associates (Cleveland),
   Architects
Miesian
A precise, stylistic delineation of contemporary buildings is not always possible; however, the symmetry, the large expanse of glass wall and the revealment of the structural frame suggest Miesian influence. There is an exquisitely furnished Treasure Room embellished by the wood carving of Cleveland's James Fillous behind the window bays to the left of the entrance.

394. Andrews Library
Front Entrance Detail
Geometric grille above the entrance bears the seal of the College "Ex Uno Fonte"—(diverse knowledge from one source). A classic-derived wave design decorates the architrave.

Other Notable Ohio Collegiate Architecture

395. Chapman Hall (1862–64)
Mt. Union College, Alliance
Simeon Porter, Architect
Romanesque Revival-Eclectic
Simeon Porter commenced his career in Hudson working in the Classic Revival style, but was introduced to the Romanesque when, circa 1850, he formed a partnership with Charles Heard. Among the better known, surviving works of this union are the Old Stone Church (Figure No. 447) on Cleveland's Public Square and College Hall (1859) on the campus of Lake Erie College, Painesville. Chapman Hall represents one of the major commissions entertained by Porter following the dissolution of the partnership.

396. Towers Hall (1870–72)
Otterbein College, Westerville
Robert T. Brooks, Architect
Eclectic
Otterbein's "Old Main" is a fanciful combination of pointed Gothic windows, a Mansardic roof and curious, picturesque towers. The college was founded 25 years earlier.

397. Dietsch Hall (1889)
Baldwin-Wallace College, Berea
Eclectic Gothic
Dietsch Hall's architect is unknown but it is assumed that it was designed and built by the competent German founders and associates of what was then German-Wallace College. Constructed of Berea sandstone, it is a curious blending of pointed Gothic elements, a central masonry wall-dormer flanked by unique "dual" dormers and a roof bordering on the Mansardic. (Cf. also Fig. #316—The College Chapel at Baldwin-Wallace)

398. Founder's Hall (1964)
Ashland College, Ashland
Lawrence Russell, Architect
Georgian Revival
At Ashland College as at Miami University, a simple derivation of Georgian forms cloaks the Administration Building which occupies a commanding position on the campus. The circular shaded patio in the foreground serves as a delightful rendevous.

399. **University Hall Tower** (1930)
University of Toledo, Toledo
Late Gothic Revival
This familiar 200 foot high tower on Bancroft Avenue, a Toledo landmark for over 40 years, has long been regarded as an outstanding example of collegiate Gothic architecture. The Walter E. Snyder Memorial Chimes (electronic) ring from its open belfrey. The adjoining wings have much in common with the Jacobethan mode.

400. **Engineering Research Building** (1969)
University of Dayton, Dayton
Pretzinger & Pretzinger, Architects (Dayton)
Contemporary
What vast stylistic and structural advances separate this from Ohio University's Cutler Hall (1816; Fig. 385). How much has been learned about new materials and new ways of building since Ohio attained statehood 170 years ago. Here we are expressing ourselves with these materials and techniques.

Architectural "Tale of Two Cities"

Cincinnati

401. **Baum-Taft House** (c. 1820)
Pike Street, Cincinnati
Attributed to Benjamin Latrobe or James
  Hoban
Federal
The Baum-Taft House, one of the finest
early residences in Ohio by any yard stick,
is believed to have been designed by either
James Hoban (White House architect) or
Benjamin Latrobe (early United States
Capitol architect). A central pavillion is
flanked by two wings. Like Monticello,
the house gives the appearance of having
a single story atop an English basement;
whereas, actually the central portion contains two full floors. The elliptical fan light
over the entrance and the oval lights below
the eaves, as well as in the pediment, are
Federal forms. The style is of southern
inspiration quite unlike the "four square"
mansions in the northeast with which it
is contemporary.

402. **Baum-Taft House**
Closeup—Portico and Facade
In 1908 President William Howard Taft
accepted the nomination for President
from this portico. Charles Phelps Taft, half
brother to the President, acquired the home
through his marriage to Anna Sinton,
daughter of David Sinton, in 1873.

403. Baum-Taft House
Rear View From Garden

Novel, triple sash windows, opening from the ballroom floor, provide access to the upper porch deck from which one may enjoy a splendid view of the garden below. The ground level, actually a basement, contains service quarters, kitchen, servant's dining room, etc. The garden was re-designed by Henry Fletcher Kenney, landscape architect, in 1949.

405. Baum-Taft House
Aspect From Entrance Hall To The Ballroom Beyond.

Known as the Taft Museum, the Baum-Taft House today houses one of America's finest private art collections. Busts of David Sinton and Anna Sinton Taft, executed by Ohioan Hiram Powers, grace the pedestals.

404. Baum-Taft House
Front Entrance Hall

The fine, Federal entranceway is a focal point of interest. Not to be overlooked, however, are the ceiling center-piece and the murals executed by the Scotch-Negro artist, Robert Duncanson, subsequent to 1830 when the home was owned by Nicolas Longworth.

407. Baum-Taft House
South Half Of The Ballroom
Throughout much of its history the Baum-Taft House has figured in Cincinnati's social life and nowhere more-so than in this gracious ballroom. The large oil painting over the sofa is Thomas Gainsborough's "Edward and William Tomkinson." High ceilings contribute to its spacious character.

406, 408. Baum-Taft House
Goya Room (To The Right Of The Entrance Hall)
The Goya Room derives its name from the artist's portrait of Queen Maria Luisa executed c. 1800 which hangs over the mantelpiece. Furnishings in the house reflect mainly the contemporary English Regency and French Directoire and Empire styles; also an important collection of Duncan Phyfe's translations of these. Mantelpiece (not necessarily original) is pure Federal—quite in keeping with the taste of the period in which the residence was built.

410. St. Peter In Chains (1841–55)
W. 8th and Plum Streets, Cincinnati
Henry Walter, Architect
Classic Revival

St. Peter in Chains would merit attention in any resume of Ohio's early church architecture. Invariably its style has been described as being "Greek Revival"; however, Renaissance forms "come through" stronger than those of the "Revival" style with which the structure was contemporary. Considering this, and since the Renaissance was essentially a rebirth of Classicism, we prefer the more inclusive label "Classic Revival." The spire, which together with the peristyle porch is the principle external feature of architectural interest, was obviously inspired by Sir Christopher Wren's and James Gibbs' work in London. The Church's plan is that of an early Italian basilica. Only a few years earlier, Henry Walter, its architect had won the competition for the design of the Ohio State House, a truly outstanding monument of the Greek Revival period. Constructed of Dayton limestone, St. Peter's measures 200 feet by 80 feet. Its tower soars to a height of 211 feet.

411. St. Peter In Chains Church
Basilica Interior

The interior of St. Peter's was remodelled in the late 1950's at which time the colorful mosaic on the chancel wall was installed (fabricated in Germany). Reredos in the south chapel is the work of Winterich Studio (Cleveland).

412. Isaac M. Wise Synagogue (1865–66)
8th and Plum Streets, Cincinnati
James K. Wilson, Architect
Eclectic-Gothic
A unique structure—not only for Ohio but for the Nation. The combined use of limestone and brick, together with the suggestion of banding, relate the style to Victorian Gothic. On the other hand, the flush arabesque sculpture and minarets hark to the Mudejar while the interior is of Byzantine character.

413. Isaac M. Wise Synagogue
Facade Detail

409. Wesley Chapel (1831) ←
5th Street near Broadway, Cincinnati
Caleb Williams, Designer
Greek Revival
The austere architecture of the Wesley Chapel is said to have been inspired by John Wesley's City Road Chapel in London. The structure is historically important since, for many years, it was the largest meeting house west of the Alleghenies. Here in 1841 the funeral services for President William Henry Harrison were held. Two years later, 76 year old ex-President John Quincy Adams delivered the dedicatory speech for a new Mt. Adams Observatory. The Chapel's continuance on this site is in limbo, but it is doubtful that its responsible corporate owners will sanction its reduction to rubble. (Notwithstanding this optimism, the Chapel was torn down in a single night in the Spring of 1972.)

414. **Music Hall** (1878)
Elm and 4th Streets, Cincinnati
Hannaford & Proctor (Cincinnati), Architects
High-Victorian Gothic

There is much that is Romanesque about Music Hall, a building which is contemporary with Richardson's Trinity Church (Boston), but there the similarity stops. The structure derives such Victorian-Gothic character as it possesses from the limestone banding and the Gothic gable forms under the traceried rose window within the central Gothic corbel arch (partially visible in this three-quarter view). This architectural type is owed largely to John Ruskin's writings of the previous quarter century, sparked by his enchantment with the Venetian Gothic. A complete restoration and modernization of Music Hall was completed in 1972 at a cost of six million dollars.

415. **The Cuvier Press Club** (1862)
22 Garfield Place, Cincinnati
Romano-Tuscan

This last remaining, town house on once sedate Garfield Place was originally occupied by the Marcus Fechheimer family. Its rectangular form, trabeated entrance and pedimented windows, all enhanced by the smooth wall surface, are characteristics of its style. The Cuvier Press Club has occupied the structure since 1937; previous to this, for some years, it was an insurance office. It is obviously the work of a competent architect.

418. **The John Hauck House** (1870)
812 Dayton Street, Cincinnati
Samuel Hannaford (?)
High-Victorian Italianate

It has only recently been ascertained that the original owner of this house was George W. Skaats, a businessman and politician whose wealth was acquired in coal mining and trade coincident with the introduction of this new fuel in the late 1850's. Hauck, who acquired the property in 1881—four years after Skaats' death—appears to have modified it extensively including the application of the impressive stone facade which we see today. Indications are that Samuel Hannaford may have been the architect. Since 1970 the house has served as headquarters of the Miami Purchase Association, a non-profit corporation founded to identify and preserve local landmarks.

416. **Bandstand** (Est. 1875)
Eden Park, Cincinnati
High-Victorian Gothic

This period-piece has to be seen at first-hand to be fully appreciated. The tile roof is, of course, red; the cast iron columns are a dark green; the wood trim, tin roof and "onion" atop it are a light green while the spandrels are painted a light yellow. The Cincinnati Art Museum may be seen on the hilltop at right.

417. Henry Probasco House (c. 1859)
North Cliff Lane, Clifton District
William Tinsley, Architect Cincinnati
Romanesque Revival
Designed for Probasco by the Irish-born architect, William Tinsley, whose other Ohio works are Ascension Hall at Kenyon College and Kokosing, both at Gambier. "The interior floor plan is ingenious: the first floor master wing is divided into four great rooms by two halls that intersect at right angles. The second floor has an octogonal central hall. The house has been called the "very embodiment of the Romantic Movement in the American Middle West."—(*Ohio Historic Landmarks:* OHS 1967) Henry Probasco was, of course, the donor of the marvelous fountain which has for almost a century been the focal point of interest on "Fountain Square."

419. Dayton Street House
North Side at Baymiller Street, Cincinnati
High-Victorian Italianate
Obviously the town house of a successful merchant or manufacturer in which a prominent High-Victorian feature is the over-scaled, paired brackets supporting the pronounced cornice. The linear drip-mouldings over the second floor, round-headed windows; also the square windows between the cornice brackets, are somewhat unusual.

421. Cincinnati City Hall (1888–93)
Cincinnati
S. Hannaford & Son, Architects
Richardsonian
Romanesque forms, rusticated masonry, contrasting color of the stone used decoratively (to enframe windows, etc.) and that for wall surfaces; all combine to impart the Richardsonian look to Cincinnati's City Hall. The tower is 250 feet in height while the dimensions of the floor plan are 332 feet × 203 feet. The interior hall and stair-well contain mosaics and stained glass windows with allegorical scenes depicting life in early Cincinnati. Samuel Hannaford also designed the Van Wormer Library at the University of Cincinnati and several Ohio courthouses.

422. Cincinnati City Hall
Entranceway Detail
Closeup of City Hall's principal entrance illustrates the decorative stone carving in designs suggestive of Louis Sullivan's work. The total conception blends originality with historicity.

420. Gutting House (c. 1872)
515 Lafayette Avenue, Cincinnati
Second Empire
An early, eye-arresting Second Empire residence in the once exclusive "Clifton District" of the Queen City.

423. Cincinnati Art Academy (1886–87)
Eden Park, Cincinati
James W. McLaughlin, Architect
Richardsonian
The entrance to the Art Academy likewise displays Richardsonian influence. Its massive tympanum and architrave dwarf the modest portal. The adjoining Art Museum, completed the same year, is also after designs by McLaughlin.

424. Rookwood Pottery (1892)
Mt. Adams, Cincinnati
William Watts Taylor, Designer
Voyseyan
The expanse of white, stucco surface; the relatively bare gables and the tendency towards banded windows suggest the influence of Charles Voysey, the innovative English architect of this period. Here were thrown some of the finest art nouveau pots, flasks and vases ever made in America. The kilns are still in tact. A fine view of the Queen City and the Ohio River are enjoyed from the back side.

425. Rookwood Pottery
Detail—Wrought Iron Gate
The main gateway to the pottery is one of the State's most artistic works in wrought iron. Atop one of two masonry posts, rooks may be seen poised on the edge of a "feeder." (Confer Gidding—Jenny Facade—Fig. 426–7)

426, 427. Giddings And Jenny Store
(c. 1900)
Fourth Street, Cincinnati
Sullivanesque
The 1968 remodelling of the facade of the Giddings And Jenny Store won an AIA Citation for "Excellence in Community Architecture." The most interesting feature of the facade, fortunately retained, is the colorful Rookwood ceramic with which the cornice and side panels are faced. Cincinnati's Rookwood Pottery produced, between 1880 and 1910, some of the Nation's finest work, in this medium, in the popular Art Nouveau mode. The Gidding and Jenny cartouche and surrounding detail is seen in greater detail in Figure No. 427.

428. Temple of Love
Mount Storm Park, Cincinnati
Classic Revival
A Greek tholos in Ohio.

429. Cincinnati Museum of Art (c. 1910)
Eden Park, Cincinnati
Garber & Woodward (Neo-Classic Portions)
Neo-Classic Revival
The principal entrance to Cincinnati's extensive Museum achieves its monumental effect from four giant, Doric columns, in antis. Original portions of the Museum, designed by James W. McLaughlin and completed in the 1880's were in the Romanesque Revival style. Robert Alonzo Taft bust is by Jacques Lipshitz, sculptor.

430. Cincinnati Museum of Art
Lobby of the Schmidlapp Wing (Within Doric columns—Fig. 429)

431. **Union Station** (1931)
Lincoln Park Drive, Cincinnati
Albert Feldheimer & Stewart Wagner, Architects
Modernistic

Cincinnati's great station, built for $41 million to handle 216 passenger trains per day, like so many of its counterparts in the Nation, is virtually deserted in this day of air travel. Behind the great arched facade there is a spacious waiting room with an oval rotunda whose walls contain murals executed by Winold Reiss conveying the commercial history of the Queen City on the Ohio. The decorated "blocks" flanking the massive proscenium are a characteristic accessory of the Modernistic style. What continuing function will be served by the station is uncertain.

432. **Netherlands-Hilton Hotel** (1930)
Carew Tower
Cincinnati
Walter W. Ahlschlager (Chicago), Architect
Modernistic

Carew Tower as seen from the recently (1969) re-developed Fountain Square at Cincinati's center. It is interesting to note that other modernistic buildings pictured herein (State Office Building, Lincoln-Leveque Tower both at Columbus, etc.) were all built within a few years of each other for the style, born in the mid-twenties, was cut short by the great depression of the 1930's and the war of the 1940's.

433. Fountain Square (1969–70)
Cincinnati
Rogers, Taliaferro, Kostritsky & Lamb, Architects
Cincinnati's "Fountain Square," redeveloped in 1969–70, is one of the most exciting urban spaces in Ohio. In this view, taken from an elevated plaza adjoining the huge new Dubois Tower (Harrison and Abramowitz, 1969) one enjoys a fine vista of the Albee Theatre's unique Palladian facade (Thomas Lamb) (New York—architect—1927. The theatre is threatened by replacement with a 50-story high-rise building as this volume goes to press.)

434. Probasco Fountain and The Dubois Tower (1969)
Fountain Square, Cincinnati
Tower by Harrison & Abramowitz, New York City
Contemporary
Eight hundred years ago man built soaring Gothic cathedrals in which to worship God; today his greatest temples are secular; but they are beautiful and they are a tribute to his ingenuity and his intelligence. Intriguing, is it not, that Henry Probasco esteemed the City in which he lived and prospered enough to provide it with such a marvelous piece of "street furniture." (Reed Miller, sculptor, 1872)

435. Fountain Square
Detail of the Fountain sculpted by Reed Miller.

438. Murray Seasongood Pavillion (1959)
Eden Park, Cincinnati
Potter, Tyler, Martin & Roth, Architects
Contemporary
Etched on it's stone proscenium is the axiom: "Enough if something from our hands have power to live and act and serve the future hour."

437. City Hall Tower
Cincinnati—From Garfield Park
A scenic vista in the heart of the City.

440. Riverfront Stadium (1970)
Cincinnati
Heery & Heery, Alexander & Rothschild (Atlanta), Architects
Contemporary
Like a giant wading pool, Cincinnati's new sports stadium is strategically located between the Ohio River and a major traffic artery.

439. Downtown Cincinnati
Scene northward on Vine Street featuring, at left, the *Central Trust Bank Building* (1913, Cass Gilbert—New York, Architect; Garber & Woodward,—Resident Architects) with pyramidal, Halicarnassus cap and, at right, the *Provident Tower* (1967, Harold Berry [Dallas], Architect).

441. "The Cloisters" (1970)
Mount Adams, Cincinnati
Hardy, Holzman & Pfeiffer (New York City), Architects
Contempory
An exciting condominium development overlooking the Ohio River on the slopes of Mount Adams—only minutes from downtown Cincinnati. The living units feature high ceilings, balcony rooms and unique spacial arrangements.

442. Bethesda Hospital (1970)
Montgomery
Smith, Hinchman & Grylls, Architects
Contemporary
Isaacs & Sullivan, Consultant Architects
(Miesian Influence)
There are many stylistic forces at work here: Miesian for its declared functionalism; Brutalist for its bulk; perhaps even Wrightian for its horizontality. Modular construction facilitates planned expansion to eventually accomodate over 1,000 beds.

443. Madiera County Library (1965)
Miami Road, Greater Cincinnati
Carl A. Strauss & Associates, Architects
Contemporary (Wrightian)
If a "prevailing horizontality" and "importance of the roof as a character-giving feature" are Wrightian forms, then there is no doubt as to the proper stylistic assignment for the Madiera Library.

444. Madiera County Library
Interior
Perforated brick divider-wall provides light and enhances the spacious character of the interior. (Entrance is at far right.)

Cleveland

BEYOND HIS PARTY
AND BEYOND HIS CLASS
THIS MAN FORSOOK THE

446. St. Theodosius Russian Orthodox Cathedral
Starkweather Ave.
Frederick Baird, Architect—Built 1911-12
This oldest Russian Orthox Church in Cleveland is considered to be one of the finest examples of its type in the United States. The large central dome, decorated with an icon of Christ on its interior surface, is surrounded by twelve subsidiary cupolas representing the apostles. Architect Baird, with the aid of photographs supplied to him, designed the building after The Church of Our Savior Jesus Christ in Moscow. In the course of a restoration during the early 1950's every inch of the large and many-faceted interior space was colorfully decorated with religious allegories by Andrew Bicenko who learned his art in Russia.

448. The Cuyahoga Building (1892)
Public Square
Burnham & Root, Architects (Chicago)
Commercial Style
Too little attention has been paid by Clevelanders, including historians, to Burnham & Root's Cuyahoga Building. It represents an architectural style which flourished in Chicago where one of its finest expressions, also by Burnham & Root, is the famous Monadnock Building which was completed only a year or two before the Cleveland project. The abundant fenestration, including particularly the offset, "Chicago windows" (three-window bays), together with the clean, uncluttereed lines and de-emphasis of the cornice, are characteristic forms. Almost totally unoccupied in its upper floors as this volume goes to print, the building's future would appear to be in great jeopardy.

447. First Presbyterian Church ("Old Stone") (1853–58; 1884)
Public Square   (*page 273*)
Heard & Porter, Architects
Romanesque Revival
"Old Stone" Church is now the oldest and most venerable building in Cleveland's central area. Originally constructed in 1853, it was rebuilt in 1858 after being badly damaged by fire. Until 1884 the East tower (right) was capped by a flêche which soared to a height of 228 ft. This was removed as being unsafe after another disastrous fire in that year when Charles Schweinfurth was called upon to conduct the restoration. The Church's interior is impressive for its trussed, wooden, barrel-vaulted ceiling; also for the curving sweep of the galleries (added in 1866). It is also enhanced by many fine stained glass windows of which several are from Louis Tiffany's New York studios. Charles Heard as a young man was apprenticed to Jonathan Goldsmith of Painesville whose daughter he married; Simeon Porter's work at Hudson is illustrated elsewhere in this volume. Their partnership lasted about a decade (1849–1859).

449, 450. **St. John's Historic Episcopal Church** (1836)
Church Avenue
Hezekiah Eldredge, Master-Builder
Cleveland
Gothic Revival

Celeveland's oldest existing church, constructed of coarse rubble-stone, has strong associations with the city's first families. Unfortunately, it loses much of its "personality" without the finials which originally capped the facade and tower tourelles. Through its portal (Fig. 450A) Daniel Pomeroy Rhodes, Marcus Hanna, D. Z. Norton and many other prominent citizens have walked.

451. The Old Arcade (1890)
Superior Avenue, Cleveland
Smith & Eisenmann, Architects
Romanesque Revival
The Arcade, considered by some to be the City's most venerable landmark, was built by a group of entrepreneurs including Myron T. Herrick, Charles F. Brush, John D. Rockefeller and L. H. Severance, who envisioned a new retail concept in the assembly of many stores under one roof where one might buy anything from an abacus to a xylophone. Today we see the rebirth of this idea in some of our great suburban shopping centers. Linking Euclid and Superior Avenues, the cavernous, glass-roofed, 300 foot long enclosure connects office buildings at either extremity. The great, segmental Superior Avenue entrance arch in our illustration remains unmolested, however the Euclid Ave. entrance was altered following World War II.

452. The Old Arcade
Interior
The design of the truss system supporting this glass roof was as novel as the spread footings, 3 feet to 8 feet square, employed to secure the foundation over the sandy soil base. John Eisenmann, co-architect, was a professor of Civil Engineering at what was then known as Case School of Applied Science.

453. Garfield Monument (1890)
Lake View Cemetery, Cleveland
George Keller (Hartford, Connecticut), Architect
Romanesque Revival
George Keller of Hartford, Connecticut, won the competition for the design of this Monument over 50 other entrants. The structure is 180 feet in height—the same as Nelson's Monument on Trafalgar Square, London—and 50 feet in diameter. The frieze scenes, depicting events in Garfield's life, are by Casper Buberl; Thomas Simmons is credited with the cut-stone and masonry work.

454, 455. Society National Bank Building
(1870)

Public Square, Cleveland
Burnham & Root, Architects
Richardsonian

The Society National Bank Building on Cleveland's Public Square is one of the last of the large buildings to be erected in the City without a complete steel structural grid. It originally contained a great, central light-well, covered by a glass skylight, which extended from the first floor upwards. This was surrounded, on each floor, by a cantilevered, open corridor providing access to the offices. The ground floor banking quarters, with murals by Louis P. Szanto and Andrew B. Karoly, are much admired. The corner lantern (Figure No. 455) has the distinction of being the first outdoor street-lighting fixture in the world (iron work by Winslow Brothers of Chicago).

456. Soldiers and Sailors Monument
(1890–94)
Public Square, Cleveland
Levi Schofield, Architect
Eclectic
The 140 ton column of black Quincy granite, extending over 100 feet skyward, is a principle feature of Schofield's monument to Cleveland's sons who served in the War Between The States. Atop it is "Liberty" personified as a woman, with a shield in one hand and a sword in the other. The sculptural groups on plinths opposite each face, honoring the four services (infantry, cavalry, artillery and navy), also designed by Schofield, are becoming increasingly respected.

457. Rockefeller Building (1903–05)
Superior Avenue at W. 6th Street, Cleveland
Knox & Elliott, Architects
Commercial Style
John D. Rockefeller personally financed this first large structural-steel, frame building on the Cleveland scene. It follows the dictum set forth by Louis Sullivan of Chicago—"form follows function." Roughly contemporary with Sullivan's Prudential Building (Buffalo) and Wainwright Building (St. Louis), Knox & Elliott's effort need make no apology to either. The bottom three floors of the facade are surfaced with quarter-inch thick cast iron plate bearing a Sullivanesque decorative design. The cornice flares gracefully outward.

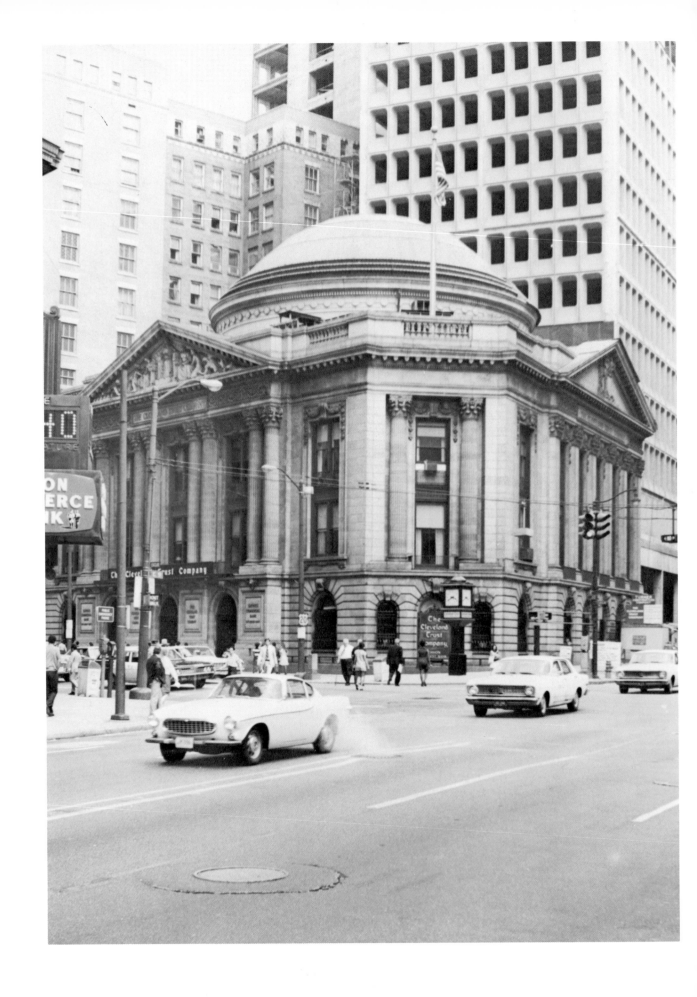

459. The Wade Chapel (1901)
Lake View Cemetery, Cleveland
Hubbell & Benes, Architects
Neo-Classic Revival
The introduction to Wade Chapel, dedicated to the memory of Cleveland industrialist, Jeptha Wade, is an experience for the person equipped by study or travel to appreciate it. Some consider it to be the most exquisite little building in Cleveland, and perhaps in the State. The exterior fabric is of light Barre granite from Vermont. To enter its trabeated threshold is to penetrate the inner recesses of a jewel: the far wall is perforated by a sizeable favrile-glass Tiffany window. Glass mosaics on the side walls, each 32 feet long and 8 feet in height, depict "The Voyage of Life"; white marble coffered ceiling, choir screen and benches—are all accented with gilted glass mosaic inlays. Builder of this too-little appreciated gem was Joseph Carabelli, Sr.

460. The Wade Memorial Chapel
Viewed From The East
Tiffany window can be seen in the rear wall. The setting befits the architecture.

458. The Cleveland Trust Company
(1909)
Euclid at E. 9th Street, Cleveland
George Post, Architect
Charles Schneider, Resident Architect
Neo-Classic Revival
Too few Clevelanders take time to appreciate the architectural beauty of this fine "temple of finance" built when the Nation's architects were still under the spell of Chicago's Columbian Exposition. Post here has made a most successful accomodation to the triangular site employing dual pedimented facades (Euclid Avenue's contains sculpture by Karl Bitters). The drum of the domed skylight (61 feet in diameter), rising 85 feet above the main banking floor, is surfaced with murals by Francis Davis Millet, depicting the commercial and industrial life of the City. The Bank is to be congratulated for recognizing the beauty and continuing usefulness of this original main office and for refraining from turning the bulldozer loose upon it when building the much-needed addition adjacent thereto (Marcel Breuer & Associates, Architect).

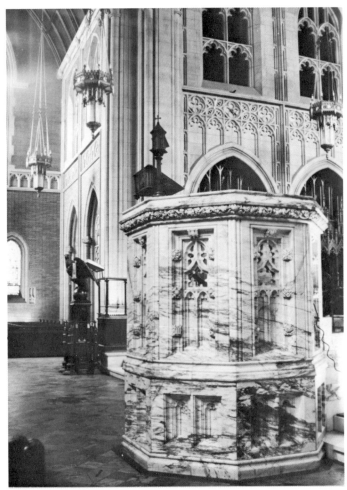

461. Trinity Cathedral (1901–07)
Euclid Avenue at 22nd Street, Cleveland
Charles Schweinfurth, Architect
Late Gothic Revival
This is the master-work of the most influential architect to practice in Cleveland between 1883 and 1910. Schweinfurth had the happy faculty of inducing his clients to raise their sights and open their pocket books—else the great tower at Trinity would never have been completed. He did not disappoint; he built solidly; he was a perfectionist who made sure that his client received full value. The original designs for Trinity Cathedral were in the Romanesque style, but ultimately the English Perpendicular Gothic prevailed.

462. Trinity Cathedral
Interior Detail
Richness of interior detail becomes apparent in the Baptismal fount at the crossing.

463. **Wade Park Bridge at Liberty Boulevard** (c. 1900)
Cleveland
Charles F. Schweinfurth, Designer

At the turn of the century, Charles Schweinfurth, then Cleveland's pre-eminent architect, was called upon to design a series of bridges across the thoroughfare now known as Liberty Boulevard. Most admired among these is that at Wade Park for the manner in which it blends into the rustic setting. It is almost obscured in spring and summer by the vines which cling to its rugged vousoirs. A particularly delightful feature of Schweinfurth's concept is the gracefully curving pedestrian stair.

464 **Cleveland City Hall** (1916)
Cleveland
J. Milton Dyer, Architect
2nd Renaissance Revival

A contemporary article commenting on the work of Clevelander Milton Dyer credited him with proficiency in a number of styles and building types; also in executing so spendid and substantial a building as Cleveland City Hall on a $3 million budget. Its most impressive space is a central, vaulted, balconied concourse extending the full height of the structure. In December of 1972 City Hall was the first building to achieve landmark status following nomination by the City's Landmark Commission legislated into existence 12 months earlier.

465. The West Side Market (1912)
Lorain Avenue at W. 25th Street, Cleveland
Hubbell & Benes, Architects
Modernistic
Main concourse of the West Side Market (at tower's base) is 241 feet in length, 124 feet in width and 44 feet in height. Its vaulted double ceiling, reinforced by five great arches and surfaced with buff colored brick in a herring bone pattern, covers one of the great covered spaces in the City. The square tower, 137 feet in height with battered walls, reminiscent of the campaniles which often adjoin medieval Italian Churches, originally provided for water storage in addition to being a neighborhood landmark.

466. West Side Market
Interior

**467. Fine Arts Garden with Cleveland
  Museum of Art**
A beauty spot which comes alive with
cherry blossoms, daffodils and people in
Spring. "Night and Day," in the fore-
ground, is by Paris-trained sculptor Frank
Jirouch, a Clevelander.

468. The Cleveland Museum of Art (1917)
University Circle,
Hubbell & Benes, Architects
Neo-Classic Revival
Cleveland's cultural roots run deep in her
schools, her library, her symphony and
her Playhouse. In 1917 her leading families—rich with the prosperity of industry
and trade—contributed the means to make
this great institution possible. Architects
Hubbell and Benes had the combined skills
to design a museum worthy of the City.

469. The Cleveland Museum of Art (1971 Addition)

Marcel Bruer/Hamilton Smith, Architects
Modern (Brutalism)

In adding to an existing building, architects have two options: to adhere to the original style; or to look forward in a new idiom. The break with tradition already made by Hays and Ruth in their 1959 addition to the Museum eased the decision confronting Marcel Breuer & Associates a decade later. Their stunning banded accretion appears to have had its inspiration in the similarly banded duomos at Florence, Sienna and Orvieto, but it is as sharp and fresh and modern as tomorrow. Its porte-cochere lunges forward like a giant arthropod. It houses new galleries and educational facilities.

470. The Cleveland Museum of Art

1971 Addition
Portion of the eastern facade including the sunken court providing access to lower level. Here, the addition's rough, marble texture and highly contrasted banding are fully apparent.

471. The Temple (1924)
University Circle, Cleveland
Charles R. Greco (Boston), Architect
Byzantine
Who has looked upon this dome from the Art Museum terrace and not been impressed with its simple geometric beauty. Unlike the Christian faiths, there is no prescribed or traditional form for a Synagogue which usually takes on the prevailing style of its place and time. Thus, one sees a Greek Revival type in Charleston S.C., a Colonial model at Newport (Rhode Island), a Victorian-Gothic specimen in Cincinnati (Confer Figure No. 412) and a strikingly contemporary design in Beechwood (Cf. Fig. 322–3) In the Temple, beyond the narthex, there is a large, hexagonal sanctuary.

472. Epworth-Euclid Church (1932)
University Circle, Cleveland
Bertram Goodhue, Architect
Late Gothic Revival
A rare Ohio work from the hand of the Gothicist, Bertram Goodhue (who passed away before its completion), viewed from the terrace of the former Garden Center of Cleveland. It is said that the architect contemplatively considered the site on foot from every aspect for the better part of a week before turning to his drawing board—and he considered it well, as the result proves. Coincidentally, there is some similarity between The Temple (Figure No. 471) and Epworth-Euclid Church: both adopt the configuration of a hexagon, but the later, with its "oil can" fleche, accentuates the vertical while the former is squat, ponderous and geometric.

474, 474A. Cleveland Institute of Music
(1961–62)
East Boulevard, Cleveland
Schafer, Flynn & Associates, Architects
Contemporary (New Formalism)
The new home of another of the distinguished cultural institutions ringing Wade Park's Cultural Garden in the University Circle area blends beautifully with the nearby traditional architecture of the Western Reserve Historical Society and the Neo-Classic Museum of Art, demonstrating that a group of buildings need not relate to each other stylistically to exist in harmony.

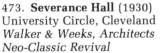
473. Severance Hall (1930)
University Circle, Cleveland
Walker & Weeks, Architects
Neo-Classic Revival
The excellence of this monumental porch has come to symbolize the perfection for which the Cleveland Orchestra is widely acclaimed. Within, one is immediately introduced to a marble-lined oval foyer with grand staircases at either end, ascending to the mezzanine. The auditorium, beyond, is warm, comfortable, conservative in its decor (cartouches by Frank Jirouch) and notable for its fine accoustics.

475. **Greater Cleveland Garden Center**
   (1965)
East Boulevard, Cleveland
William & Geoffrey Platt, Architects
Schafer, Flynn Associates, Architects
Clark & Rapuano, Landscape Architects
Contemporary (Wrightian)
If there is a finer Garden Center in the Nation than Cleveland's, we are unaware of it. Here the sons of Charles A. Platt (Figure No. 124) and the talented landscape architects, Clark and Rapuana (Figure No. 487) have combined their talents in creating a truly outstanding center whose basic purpose—in tune with the 1970's—is environmental improvement. Photo portrays the west facade, patio and lily ponds.

476. **Greater Cleveland Garden Center**
Motor entrance to underground garage from East Boulevard. Large high-profile, single-story wing at left, with opposing glass walls, is used for exhibits and lectures.

480. St. James Church (c. 1932) →

17514 Detroit Avenue, Cleveland
E. T. P. Grahm, Architect
Saracenic Romanesque
Built in the depths of the Great Depression of the 1930's, St. James Catholic Church can rightfully take pride in the rich artistry and decor of its nave and chancel—too little known and appreciated by Clevelanders. To enter this Church is to enter a museum of ecclesiastical art expressed in stained glass, in carved wood, in a variety of imported marbles and one of the finest painted ceilings in America by David Scott Brown and Karl W. Schubert.

478, 479. Shaker Square (1930)
Cleveland
Phillip Small, Architect
Georgian Revival
"Shaker Square," believed to be the earliest shopping center in Cleveland and in Ohio, remains the most aesthetically pleasing of all that have followed. It consists of four quadrants, much like the one pictured, whose varying roof lines contribute to its charm. The Cleveland Trust Co. facade (Figure No. 479) illustrates the Georgian detailing.

477. **Cultural Gardens** (1920's)
East Boulevard, Cleveland
Few cities in America have drawn more deeply than Cleveland from the many nationalities of Europe: Irish came early to build the canal and man the lake boats; Poles and Slavs and Czeks were attracted by her heavy industry; Hungarians and Ukranians worked her garment factories; German girls were attracted by oppotunities in domestic work, etc. All are represented in the Cultural Gardens which for several miles line East Boulevard—a unique Cleveland asset.

481. **St. James Church**
Entrance Detail
Entrance to St. James is gained from a triple-arched porch, supported by monolithic, marble columns, through bronze doors decorated in low relief with symbols of the Evangelists.

483. **Federal Reserve Bank Building**
Banking Concourse
Banking concourse of the Federal Reserve Bank, lined throughout with Siena marble, is the richest interior in the central City. Dome on pendentives at the head of the entrance stair is circumferentially inscribed with the names of the twelve Federal Reserve districts.

482, 482A. **Federal Reserve Bank of Cleveland** (1923)
Superior at E. 6th Street, Cleveland
Walder & Weeks, Architects
Second Renaissance Revival
Of the many major works carried out in Cleveland by Walker & Weeks, none exceeds the Federal Reserve Bank in beauty of design, or in the quality of workmanship and materials used. The exterior walls of this Renaissance palace are faced, from sidewalk to cornice, with a soft, pink Georgian, Etowah granite. The entablature of the tabernacle entrance (illustrated in Fig. #482A) is embellished with bronze metopes in the image of ancient Roman coins. Flanking it are personifications of "Integrity" (left) and "Security" (right) by the New York sculptor, Henry Herring.

484. **Federal Reserve Bank Building**
Detail
Bronze "Energy" by Henry Herring beside Superior Avenue entrance.

485. Mall Vista with New Federal Building (1968) *(opposite top)*
9th Street at Lakeside, Cleveland
Outcalt-Guenther/Shafer-Flynn/Dalton & Dalton—in Association, Architects
Miesian
Cleveland War Memorial Fountain (1955–56), at the south end of the Mall (Marshall M. Fredericks, sculptor), provides foreground interest for the new, stainless steel sheathed Miesian Federal Building.

486. Terminal Tower (1929) and **Mall War Memorial** *(lower left)*
Cleveland
Grahm, Anderson, Probst & White were the architects of The Terminal Tower, a monument to the fabulous Van Sweringen's vast railroad empire. New York Central's passenger trains were electrified and re-routed around the City in order to enter its subterranean station which rivalled New York's Grand Central Terminal in size if not in beauty. Here the Tower, for four decades the tallest building between New York and Chicago, is seen from the Mall through the haze of a midsummer day.

487. Hanna Plaza—"The Mall"
(Completed 1964) *(lower right)*
Cleveland
Clark & Rapuano (New York City), Designers
Clevealnd has developed in the post World War II period and there is much that is beautiful in the "Forest City" if one will look about. Foremost among such sights, in the heart of the City, is Hanna Plaza at the northern end of The Mall—a late dividend of the City's far-seeing "Group Plan."

489. Jewish Community Federation (1965)
1750 Euclid Avenue, Cleveland
Edward Durrell Stone, Designer
Contemporary (New Formalism)
First and prime example in the central city of the "New Formalist" style. Here "columnar supports tend to be thicker and more fully modelled than in the International and Miesian styles, while the arch, absent from the others, may constitute the ruling motif of the design."* The projecting slab of the flat roof (cornice) is likewise, a prominent feature.
*From *American Architecture Since 1780*—Marcus Whiffen

488. No. 1 Erieview Plaza (Center) →
(Completed in 1967)
Federal Building (Right) (Completed in 1966)
East 9th Street, Cleveland
Architect, No. 1 Erieview Plaza—Schaefer, Flynn & Associates
Architects, Federal Building—
Schaefer, Flynn & Williams)
Outcault-Guenther) In Association
Dalton & Dalton)
Miesian
Lake Erie lies beyond these Miesian structures forming a portion of the Erieview re-development of downtown Cleveland. They are seen here from the steps of St. John's Cathedral. Facing them beyond a terrace and fountain pond—is Erview Plaza (Harrison & Abramowitz), first and largest building in this grandioise urban design.

490. Science Building (1970)
Cleveland State University, Cleveland
Outcalt, Rode, Kaplan & Curtiss, Architects
Contemporary
Patio before Seience Building provides a convenient campus rendevous. The structure combines elements of the Miesian and New Formalist styles. The founding of a great State University at Cleveland's heart is the most promising urban development of the entire post-war period. It is anticipated that it will function as a great magnet bringing people and life to the City's center.

492. Cuyahoga Community College
  (1969–70)
Cleveland
Outcalt, Rode, Kaplan & Curtiss, Architects
Contemporary
A portion of the "student court" is seen in this photo while the Terminal Tower, at the heart of Cleveland, looms in the distance. Multi-level plan adds visual interest to the inner campus which may be circum-pre-ambulated at this balcony level. Cuyahoga Community College and Cleveland State University are comparatively new institutions which planners anticipate will add new vitality to the city center. Building at far end of "court" is the college library.

491. University Tower (1971)
22nd Street at Chester Avenue, Cleveland
Outcalt, Rode, Kaplan & Curtiss (Cleveland), Architects
Contemporary
High-rise structure formally known as The Library and Faculty Office Building, is the nerve center and most visible landmark of the new Cleveland State University founded (from Fenn College) in the late 1960's. Brutalist building in the foreground (1970, Dalton, Dalton & Little) is the University Lecture Center and Academic Building. (Cf. also #508—University Hall—CSU's Student Union.)

493. Grant Elementary School (1969)
Warren Road, Lakewood
Robert A. Little—George F. Dalton & Associates, Architects
Contemporary
A far cry from the "little red schoolhouse," but in another sense not so far, since here—in keeping with modern teaching theory—as many as four classes may be held in their respective corners of one huge room. "Open construction" permits rooms of differing function to flow into one another often without partition. Mansard roof carried, ad absurdum, suggests the Second Empire revived! This design has come in for much favorable comment both by architects and educators.

494. Reception Center—Nela Park
  (1968–69)
Noble Road, Cleveland
Visnapu & Gaede, Architects
Contemporary (Wrightian)
A striking new reception center "in-the-round" for an established Cleveland institution. Low profile, circular design and roofline emphasis place it in the Wrightian category. An important feature in the design is the terne metal fascia employed for its adaptability to the structure's curving form.

495. Reception Center—Nela Park
Interior view illustrates the formal, informality achieved. Floor is a concrete slab; brick piers are reinforced by the structural steel frame.

498. Advertising Building (1911–13)
Nela Park, Cleveland
Wallace & Goodwillie (NYC), Architects
Georgian Revival
The 37 acre site for NELA park, one of the very first research and/or industrial parks to be established in the Nation, was selected in 1910. Obviously, noting its date, the subject was among the first buildings to have been completed. Its Georgian forms (pedimented entrance porch, lateral pavillions with segmental pediments, acroteria and roof-top ballustrade), borrowed from English proto-types, are seen in many a country manor-house in that country. Wallace & Goodwillie designed all building at NELA Park through 1923.

497. Stouffer's "Pier W" Restaurant
(1965)
Edgewater Boulevard, Lakewood
Romweber-Bornhorst, Architects
Contemporary
A novel and posh place to dine while cantilevered over Lake Erie's shore with Cleveland's skyline in the distance—creating the illusion that one is "at sea."

496. High-Rise Apartments (c. 1969)
On Cleveland's "Gold Coast"
During the 1960's, after a long hiatus, people were once again attracted to Cleveland's lake shore as a place to live—in view of downtown and colorful sunsets. Here, nestled in the foreground cliff, Stouffer's fashionable "Pier W" Restaurant protrudes like a ship's prow.

499. Blossom Music Center (1968)
Steel Corner Road, Bath Township
Schafer, Flynn & Van Dijk (Cleveland),
Architects
Contemporary
Summer home of the Cleveland Orchestra
and one of the Nation's foremost pavillions
for the enjoyment of music in a natural
setting. A giant steel parabolic arch is the
structural "backbone" of the design. Accoustics are such that "picnicers" can relax
anywhere on the vast lawn while enjoying
a concert.

500. Holden Arboretum Thayer Center
    (1965)
Kirtland
John Terrence Kelley, Architect
Contemporary (Wrightian)
Several prominent Cleveland families
donated their estates east of Cleveland to
form this haven for nature lovers. In 1965
Cleveland architect John Terrence Kelley
was called upon to design the Thayer
(reception) Center thereon which is
Wrightian for its horzontality and the importance given to the roof as a "character-
giving feature." It is situated on the edge
of a pond dimly visible at the right.

501. University School (1970)
Hunting Valley
Flynn, Dalton, Van Dijk & Partners (Cleveland), Architects
Contemporary
The architects have here done a superlative job in adapting a building to a lovely wooded site. In accordance with the newest ideas in school planning, the principal functioning parts of the structure (auditorium, cafeteria, library, etc.) are not separated by walls from each other, but rather their spaces are continuous, flowing "openings" from the central hall. The interior, concrete wall surfaces reflect the grained pattern of the wood against which they were cast. Within and without, the building is a visual encounter with bold geometric forms.

502. University School
Aspect From Corridor-Lounge Eastward
Expanses of glass never allow the occupant to lost sight of the surrounding, natural beauty. Extending wing seen in this photo houses the cafeteria on the ground floor and the library-study area on the cantilevered second story.

503, 504. The Temple Branch (1970)
Shaker Boulevard, West of Brainard,
 Cleveland
Perkin & Will (Chicago), Architects
Contemporary
An elongated, contemporary porte-cochere together with a "staircase" roof are the principal stylistic features of The Temple Branch. The covered walkway encloses a pleasant, cobblestone-surfaced patio observable at the extreme left. The complex's visible mass contains a large auditorium and assembly hall. Fig. 504 illustrates the garden-patio fronted by the porte-cochere.

**507. Clanonberry Court—Daisy Hill
 Farms** (1927)
Hunting Valley   *(top right)*
George Brown, Stonemason
(Cleveland Environs)
French Provincial
The landscaping, as well as the spotting of the bridges, towers and walls at the Van Sweringen Brother's fabulous Daisy Hill Farms, was planned by landscape architect William Taylor. However, George Brown, the talented Gates Mills stonemason, was called upon to execute the structural elements. This ensemble of tower, bridge and retaining wall before the formerly well-stocked "Van" stables— looking more like rural Normandy than northeast Ohio—is typical of the best of his work.

506. American Society for Metals
Detail of Buckminster Fuller's geodesic dome at Newbury.

505. American Society for Metals (1964)
Route 87, Newbury
Buckminster Fuller, Design
(Cleveland Environs)
Geodesic Dome
Appropriately, the American Society for Metals chose an aluminum geodesic dome to accent its headquarters in rural Geauga County—some twenty miles east of Cleveland's Public Square. The stunning inner "court" contains a saucer-shaped basin with fountain.

508. **University Hall**—Cleveland State
   University (1910)
2605 Euclid Ave.
Charles F. Schweinfurth, Architect
Jacobethan Revival
This last and most expensive of the great
mansions to have been built on Euclid
Avenue was designed by Cleveland's then
preeminent architect for Samuel Mather,
one of the City's most influential citizens.
The stylistic designation is owed, in part,
to the stone, mullioned window bays and
multiple chimney pots. For many years
the headquarters of the Cleveland Auto
Club; the great house now serves as a
Student Union for Cleveland State University.

509. **"Shoreby"** (c. 1895)
Lake Shore Blvd., Bratenahl
Charles F. Schweinfurth, Architect
Eclectic
Architect Schweinfurth earlier designed
this lake-shore residence for his mentor,
Samuel Mather.

510A. Erieview Plaza (1964)
Cleveland
Harrison & Abramowitz, Architects
I. M. Pei, Design Concept
Contemporary
Photo illustrates the heart of Erieview Plaza with the lower portion of 100 Erieview Plaza (sometimes popularly known as the "Jolly Green Giant") in the right background. The exterior design concept for the structures at left was set by I. M. Pei, architect and planner of New York City, during the 1950's. Textured pavement surrounds a depressed fountain-pond which doubles as a skating rink in the winter-time. The establishment of Erieview Plaza, so far removed from the traditional hub of the City at Public Square, has created two, separate commercial focal points in the downtown area—a not altogether happy circumstance.

Cleveland

Urban Redevelopments

Canton

510. Central Plaza (c. 1966)
Market Street, Canton   *(below)*
Tarapata & McMahon, Architects/John John & Roy, Landscape
In the mid-1960's Canton turned an enlargement of Market Street—its main north-south thoroughfare—into a Plaza at the heart of the city. Fountains, plantings, patio and combined reception center-sandwich bar combine to create an inviting, shaded open-space in which to pass the noon hour, to rendevous and, in the winter, to ice skate (area beyond the enclosure).

Toledo

511. Levis Square (1970)
Summit Between Madison and Jefferson
  Avenues, Toledo
*Richards, Bauer & Moorhead (Toledo) in
  assoc. w. Richard K. Webel (NYC)*
Toledo's Levis Square, another exciting
central city re-development, nestles between soaring Fiberglas Tower (1969; Harrison & Abromowitz) at its southern extremity and the equally new Toledo Edison
Building on the north. Its presence adds
a welcome open-space at the City's heart
(Photo conveys the scene viewed from the
base of Fiberglas Tower—Toledo's tallest
building). The reader's attention is directed to the fountain and attractive street
lamps.

Akron

512, 513. Cascade Plaza (1970)
Main Street, Akron
Knoerle-Gould Associates, Architects
Lawrence Halperin & Associates, Land-scape Architects

Joining the parade to the city beautiful, Akron's Cascade Plaza commenced to "take shape" in the early summer of 1970. It spans the terrain once traversed by canal boats toting produce and passengers between Lake Erie and the Ohio River. Building in the photograph—one of several major architectural elements—is known as "Cascade Number III." Before it, up the foreground ramp, there is a sizeable "theatre-arena" which doubles as an ice rink in the winter. (Confer Figure No. 513) A giant metal sculpture by Akron's Don Drum adds a splendid, artistic element to the total ensemble.

Columbus' German Village

514. German Village (1960's)
Columbus

Columbus was an early mecca for German folk who built solidly in brick. Recognizing the inherent charm of their erstwhile neighborhood—and its proximity to the City's center—in the early to mid-1960's a few preservation-minded individuals commenced to promote it as a pleasant and convenient place to live. The idea "caught on!" People from all walks of life, also appreciating its possibilities, purchased properties which they then proceeded to restore and beautify. In the meantime entrepeneurs added all the urban amenities (restaurants, taverns, ice cream parlor, etc.) Thus a declining section of the city has once again become a very desirable place to live and to visit. The photo illustrates "Village" headquarters at 624 S. 3rd Street.

Roscoe Village

517, 518. Roscoe Village (1833, 1970)
Old Warehouse
Coshocton

The Ohio and Erie Canal had been open less than a year when this warehouse was built along its bank to serve the local needs. Occupying a choice location by a canal bridge, it rests on a basement lined with solid ashlars—recently converted into the charming "Warehouse Restaurant." It is an eclectic building of considerable pretention (considering its use) curiously combining a Palladian window, flanked by a split fan-light of Federal derivation, with Greek forms predominant at the time it was built. Figure No. 518 illustrates other nearby structures being restored in the recreation of Roscoe Village (1970).

Cincinnati

516. **Dayton Street Renewal** (1970) ←
Dayton Street, Cincinnati
Miami Purchase Association, 812 Dayton
  Street,—Promoters
Cincinnati's "millionaire's row" of the late
19th century has many elegant town-
houses which are being preserved and
restored for their historic and architectural
value. The finest of these, the former John
Hauck House, is reproduced in Figure No.
418.

516A. **Fountain Square,** Cincinnati
Other aspects of this exciting space at the
Queen City's center may be observed on
page 268 (Figs. 433, 434, 435)

515. **German Village**
Columbus
Typical Village vista along Sycamore
Street west of South High Street.

Notable Bridges

519. **Ohio River Suspension Bridge**
(1856–66)
Cincinnati
John A. Roebling, Engineer
Until New York's Brooklyn Bridge was built in 1883 (1,595 feet), the Cincinnati Suspension Bridge (1,057 feet) was the longest in the world—exceeding Brunel's pace-setter across the Avon at Bristol, England (1831–64), by several hundred feet. As originally constructed the bridge provided for two carriage roads, two pedestrian lanes and a double street-car track. It was remodelled in the late 1890's.

520, 521. **Germantown Covered Bridge**
(1870)
Germantown
The Germantown Bridge is believed to be the only existing inverted, bow-string truss, covered bridge in the world. It was moved from its original location, spanning Little Twin Creek on the Dayton Pike, to the present site in 1911. Figure No. 521 illustrates the unique construction of this bridge.

522. **"Y" Bridge** (1900)
Zanesville, Viewed From Putnam Hill Park.
Another unique Ohio Bridge is the "Y" at Zanesville—the third of its type on the site. Where else can one be directed to "Turn left at the middle of the bridge and proceed straight on." The Licking and Muskingum Rivers converge at the bridge.

523. Interurban Bridge (1908)
Waterville
J. M. Walker, Chief Eng.
When completed this was believed to be
the largest reinforced concrete bridge in
the world. It is composed of 12 spans 85'
to 100' in length. 12' wide piers are set
3' in solid rock. The limestone outcrop-
ping on which two of the central piers
rest is the famous Roche de Bout—historic
meeting place of the Indians where plans
were made to engage Gen. Harmar and
after him Generals St. Clair and Anthony
Wayne ("Fallen Timbers"). The bridge was
recently placed on the National Register
of Historic Places.

524. High Level Bridge (1917)
Cleveland
When completed in 1917, Cleveland's
High Level Bridge (591 feet) vied only with
New York City's "Hell Gate" (crossing the
East River) for the honor of being the
longest, steel-arch bridge in the United
States. Its lower "road bed" was designed
to handle street-cars while the upper level
carried vehicular traffic. It is viewed here
from the old (1870's) Detroit-Superior via-
duct which it replaced. Below is an old
Center Street swing bridge on the site of
the earliest bridging of the Cuyahoga River
(c. 1836).

525. "S" Bridge on the National Pike (Old
  U.S. Route 40)
West of Zanesville
During much of the 19th century the National Pike was the principal east-west
thoroughfare across Ohio's mid-section.
The Historical Marker seen in the photo
explains that the "S" shape came about
because it was easier to construct a bridge
at right angles to the direction of the creek
flow. These well-built bridges have mar-
velously withstood the ravages of time.

Bibliography

American Buildings and Their Architects: The Colonial and Neo-Classic Styles by William H. Pierson Jr. Doubleday & Co. (1970) Garden City, N.y.

A comprehensive, scholarly, yet easily readable account of the building art in America—and its practitioners—during the Colonial and Classic Revival periods (i.e. to circa 1850) interpreted from the vantage point of 1970.

America Building and the Historical Forces that Shaped It by James Marston Fitch (Revised 1966) Houghlin-Mifflin Co., Publishers

A very useful and interesting volume which concerns itself largely with the historical forces, trends and ideas which fostered neo-Classicism, the other numerous revivals and the eclecticism which marked the development of American architecture during the 19th century; also the currents and the personalities that have shaped contemporary urban building in America.

Images of American Living: Four Centuries of Architecture and Furniture as Cultural Expression by Alan Gowans (1964) J. B. Lippincott, Publishers (Third Printing)

A splendid work which traces the development of American architecture—and the American home—in great detail from its medieval origins to the present era. Handsomely illustrated.

American Architecture Since 1780: A Guide to the Styles by Marcus Whiffen (1969) MIT Press, Publishers

A very useful guide to the identification of architectural styles in America from the Revolutionary period to the present moment. Forty separate styles are grouped chronologically, described and illustrated. A handy book to have available when "building watching" in conjunction with the book in hand.

Victorian Architecture by Robert Furneaux Jordon (1966) Penguin Books Pelican Book No. A836

A brilliant review of the romantic movement in England detailing the historical background which nourished the Gothic Revival; also the influence of John Ruskin and William Morris (Arts and Crafts Movement) which so greatly affected stylistic trends on American shores.

Greek Revival Architecture in America by Talbot Hamlin Oxford University Press (1944) Dover Publications, Inc. N.Y. Reprint 1964

The definitive exposition of the Greek Revival in America

A Concise History of Western Architecture by Robert Furneaux Jordan (1970) Harcourt, Brace World, Publishers

An excellent, general history of Western architecture from ancient Greece to Frank Lloyd Wright, LeCorbusier and Mies Van der Rohe. Highly readable; well illustrated.

Architecutre of the Northwest Territory by Rexford Newcomb University of Chicago Press (1950)

This volume remains a good source of information relating to the settlement of the Northwest Territory; also the historical and geographic forces which shaped its architecture to the mid-nineteenth century. Two chapters are largely devoted to early Ohio building.

Architecture of the Western Reserve: 1800–1900 by Richard N. Campen—Press of Case Western Reserve Univ. (1971)

A comprehensive study of this heretofore, too-little noted region of northeast Ohio. The accompanying essay provides an introduction to the architectural styles encountered therein during the 19th century; also a glossary of architectural terms.

The Rise of An American Architecture edited by Edgar Kaufman Jr. Praeger Publishers (1970)

A compilation of important, incisive essays on the contribution of 19th and early 20th century America to the history of architecture and city planning.

Ohio College Architecture Before 1870 by Eric Johannesen Historic Ohio Building Series #1 Ohio Historical Society

Victorian Architect: Life and Work of William Tinsley by J. D. Fobes, University of Indiana Press

History of Ohio by Roseboom and Weisenberger Prentiss-Hall, N.Y., Publishers (1934)

The Buckeye Country by Harlan Hatcher Putnam & Sons, N.Y., Publisher (1940)

Thomas Worthington: Father of Ohio Statehood by Alfred B. Sears Ohio State University Press (1958)

*   *   *   *   *

*Forty American Architectural Styles isolated and
defined in
American Architecture
Since 1780: A Guide to the Styles**
By Marcus Whiffen   MIT Press (1969)

1. Styles that reached their Zenith in 1780–1820
   The Adam Style
   Jeffersonian Classicism) Federal Period

2. Styles that Reached their Zenith in 1820–1860
   The Greek Revival
   The Egyptian Revival
   The Early Gothic Revival
   The Romanesque Revival
   The Italian Villa Style
   The Renaissance Revival: Romano-Tuscan Mode
   The Renaissance Revival: North Italian Mode
   The Octogon Mode

3. Styles that Reached Their Zenith 1860–1890
   High Victorian Gothic
   High Victorian Italianate
   The Second Empire Style
   The Stick Style
   The Queen Anne Style
   The Eastlake Style
   The Shingle Style
   The Richardsonian Romanesque
   Chateauesque

4. Styles that Reached Their Zenith in 1890–1915
   Beaux Arts Classicism
   The Second Renaissance Revival
   The Georgian Revival
   The Neo-Classic Revival
   The Late Gothic Revival
   The Jacobethan Revival
   The Commercial Style
   Sullivanesque
   The Prairie Style
   The Western Stick Style
   The Mission Style
   Bungaloid

5. Styles That Reached Their Zenith 1915–1945
   The Spanish Colonial Revival
   The Pueblo Style
   Modernistic
   International Style

6. Styles That Have Flourished Since 1945
   Miseian
   The New Formalism
   Wrightian
   Neo-Expressionism
   Brutalism

*Reproduced with express consent of The MIT Press

Partial Listing of Ohio County Courthouses
Their dates, their architects, their style

County	Seat	Date	Architect	Style
*Allen	Lima	1882	G. Maetzel	2nd Empire
Ashtabula	Jefferson	1850/91	J. Woolly	Eclectic
*Athens	Athens	1880	H. E. Myers	Hi-Vict.—Ital.
*Auglaize	Wapakonets	1893	Kremer & Hart	2nd Ren. Rev.
*Brown	Georgetown	c1851	Hubbard Baker	Gr. Rev.
*Carroll	Carrollton	1885	Frank Weary	Eclectic
*Clinton	Wilmington	1916	Werner & Adkins	Ren. Rev. 2nd
*Columbiana	Lisbon	1871	H. E. Myer	Italianate
*Coshocton	Coshocton	1875	Carpenter/Williams	2nd Empire
Crawford	Bucyrus	1857	O. S. Kinney	Ren Rev.
Cuyahoga	Cleveland	1906–16	Lehman & Schmidt	2nd Rev. Rev.
*Delaware	Delaware	1868	R. N. Jones	Italianate
*Fayette	Washington CH	1884	D. W. Gibbs	Eclectic
*Fairfield	Lancaster	1871	Blaire/Ebner	Italianate
Franklin	Columbus	1885	G. Maetzel	2nd Empire
Gallia	Gallipolis	1876	T. S. Ford	2nd Empire
*Geauga	Chardon	1869	Jos. Ireland	Italianate
*Greene	Xenia	c1900	S. Hannaford	Richardsonian
*Guernsey	Cambridge	1881	J. W. Yost	Eclectic
*Henry	Napoleon	1880	D. W. Gibbs	2nd Empire
*Highland	Hillsboro	1834	unknown	Federal (Trans)
Holmes	Millersburg	1885	J. W. Yost	Eclectic
*Jefferson	Steubenville	1871	Heard & Blythe	2nd Empire
*Knox	Mt. Vernon	1855	Daniel Clark	Gr. Rev.
*Lake	Painesville	1907	J. M. Dyer	Beaux Arts
*Licking	Newark	1876	H. E. Myer	2nd Empire
*Lucas	Toledo	1894	Sidney Stine	Beaux Arts
*Madison	London	1890	G. Maetzel	2nd Empire
*Mahoning	Youngstown	1910	Owsley/Boucherle	2nd Ren. Rev.
*Marion	Marion	1884	D. W. Gibbs	Eclectic
Medina	Medina	1840/73	T. D. Allen	2nd Empire
*Miami	Troy	1888	J. W. Yost	Beaux Arts
*Miegs	Old Chester	1823	A. Chase, bldr.	Federal
*Miegs	Pomeroy	1847	unknown	Eclectic
*Montgomery	Dayton	1850	H. Daniels	Greek Rev.
*Morgan	Connelsville	1858	Wm. P. Johnson	Eclectic
*Ottowa	Port Clinton	1899	Wing/Mahurin	Roman. Rev.
*Perry	Somerset	1829	J. Hampson, bldr	Federal
*Pickaway	Circleville	1888–90	Weary & Kremer	Eclectic
*Putnam	Ottawa	1913	F. L. Packard	2nd Ren. Rev.
*Richland	Mansfield	1968	Thos. Zaugg etal	Contemp.
Sandusky	Fremont	1840/1935	Cyrus Williams	Neo-Classic
Shelby	Sidney	1881	G. Maetzel	2nd Empire
Stark	Canton	1895	G. F. Hammond	2nd Ren. Rev.
Summit	Akron	1906	J. M. Dyer	2nd Ren. Rev.
Trumbull	Warren	c1895	Labelle/French	Roman. Rev.
*Tuscarawas	New Phila.	1882	Thos. Boyd	Beaux Arts
Van Wert	Van Wert	1876	Thos. Tolan	2nd Empire
*Warren	Lebanon	c1836/1895	unknown	2nd Ren. Rev.
*Washington	Marietta	1901	S. Hannaford	2nd Ren. Rev.
*Wayne	Wooster	1878	Thos. Boyd	2nd Empire
Williams	Bryan	1881	E. O. Follis	
Wood	Bowling Green	1893	Yost & Packard	Richardsonian

*Indicates pictured in this volume.

Ren. Rev. = Renaissance Revival
compiled by R. N. Campen

Architect's Index

Architects and Builders whose works are represented herein

Photo Index

Photographs Opening Page—Hale Homestead

Cleveland Marking Key
*signifies an HABS Building
+ designated by Cleveland Landmarks Commission